EDDIE TRUNK'S
ESSENTIAL
HARD ROCK AND
HEAVY METAL
VOLUME II

FOREWORD BY SLASH

ABRAMS IMAGE, NEW YORK

CONTENTS

FOREWORD

Even though he is the host of VH1 Classic's *That Metal Show*, Q104.3's *Eddie Trunk Rocks*, and SiriusXM radio's *Eddie Trunk Live*, it's not Eddie Trunk's ambition that has made him a household name; it's the fact that he's one of those very rare rock-and-roll fans who has taken his all-consuming fixation on heavy metal and somehow made it a full-time career. He has combined his seemingly endless knowledge of his favorite music with the patience and stamina to learn ALL the records, ALL the songs, and ALL the players. Let's face it, he knows EVERYTHING. Eddie sincerely loves the sounds, rhythms, volume, and energy that are hard rock and heavy metal—as well as all the little details of how the music comes together and about the personalities that create it. Eddie also has the drive and the perseverance to tirelessly communicate his obsession to the world—his only motivation being the desire to share the music and the facts with other fans who care as much as he does.

I've spent a lot of time with Eddie, over many years, discussing our favorite artists. We share a love for Aerosmith and Cheap Trick, and I've witnessed Eddie go on for hours about UFO! His sincerity and genuine passion for the music always make me glad that he is a spokesman for the broad spectrum of material out there and an unbiased crusader in support of the cause. This has made Eddie an icon and a hero to artists and fans alike. We all love him.

This book is my good friend Eddie Trunk's latest installment in his endless journey through all things rock. It is an encyclopedia of loud guitars, histrionic vocals, and pounding rhythm sections that only he could write. Even when you think you've heard it all, Eddie uncovers a piece of trivia or some deep cut that you can't imagine life without. *Volume II* is a must-have for true hard rock and heavy metal purists everywhere.

—Slash, 2013

ABOVE: Slash and Eddie
OPPOSITE: Slash

INTRODUCTION

It is a huge thrill for me to present my second book, *Eddie Trunk's Essential Hard Rock and Heavy Metal, Volume II*, to my fellow rock fans and metal supporters. I hope you find that this book lives up to the great volume II's of the music world: *Led Zeppelin II*, Kiss *Alive II*, *Van Halen II* . . . well, you get the idea! I learned so much over the last few years since my first book was released, and I was truly blown away by the amazing response to it from music fans everywhere. I had always wanted to write a book, but I hadn't known what to expect, and the process was new every step of the way. I really enjoyed sharing information about my favorite bands and also telling some stories about my times with them over the years. There will never be enough pages to say everything I'd like to about music, but I'm very happy to pick up where I left off with *Volume II*.

My first book was launched with a great party at the Hard Rock Cafe in Times Square in New York City, and some of the artists featured in the book (and even some in this one) turned up along with my family and friends to toast its release. But one of the best parts of publishing the book was getting to do signings and events where I was able to connect with the fans and thank them in person for all the support they have given me. I want to thank all the wonderful people who came out to meet me—at bookstores and record stores; on rock cruises; on the grounds of the first U.S. Big Four concert, in Indio, California; and at Rocklahoma, the M3 Rock Festival, and other gigs across the country—as well as the bookstores and venues that hosted events, and the media that reviewed my book and helped it to reach the music lovers who have made it all possible. (It was fun to have the tables turned and be the one getting interviewed for a change!)

TOP: Doug Aldrich, Zakk Wylde, Sammy Hagar, Eddie, Michael Schenker, and John 5
OPPOSITE TOP: Eddie, Brad Whitford, and Zakk Wylde
OPPOSITE MIDDLE TOP: Eddie and Steven Tyler
OPPOSITE MIDDLE BOTTOM: Eddie and Rob Zombie
OPPOSITE BOTTOM: Lita Ford, Eddie, and David Coverdale
OPPOSITE RIGHT: Eddie hosting the Monsters of Rock cruise

TOP: Jim Florentine, Eddie,
Mike Portnoy, Bobby "Blitz" Ellsworth,
and Don Jamieson
MIDDLE: The marquee of the
Hard Rock Cafe in Times Square
on the night of Eddie's book launch
BOTTOM: Steven Adler
RIGHT: Jimmy Page and Eddie

One of the things people enjoyed so much about my first book was the format. Readers loved all the great photos by my friend Ron Akiyama and the others who contributed, along with the stories, playlists, and trivia. So, I've stuck with the same format this time. However, I should note that, just like in the first book, my playlists often intentionally leave out the major hit songs from the artists. (Space is always an issue in a book, so I didn't feel the need to tell everyone to check out "Welcome to the Jungle" by Guns N' Roses or "Crazy Train" by Ozzy Osbourne.) Instead, I tried to include ten tracks per band that are "deeper cuts," along with some hits that I love too much to leave out. The discographies are also incomplete. While all studio albums are included, I've listed only what I consider to be key live recordings and have left out compilations. Also because of space restrictions, not every member of bands that have had many lineup changes is represented here. Additionally, this book gave me the opportunity to explore full chapters on the bands featured in the "More Essentials" section of volume one, along with some others. Again, space is limited, so I must stress how difficult it was to choose the featured bands, and none of these selections is meant to slight the other great bands that deserve the full treatment. But like in everything I do in TV and radio, I try to present a balance of bands from both hard rock and heavy metal. If I could write about all the bands or songs that fans have stopped me to talk about on the street or in an airport or outside a concert, I would. It has been fun delving into some of the more obscure or underappreciated groups while writing this volume, and if I didn't get to a much-loved band here, I hope to do it in the future.

Hard rock and metal fans are the most loyal supporters in the world. Thank you all for listening to me on the radio for thirty years, watching *That Metal Show*, and reading these pages. I hope my two books will inspire readers to go check out a song or an album by a band they didn't know much about before and spread the word, or to enjoy learning more about one of their favorites. I hope to see you out on the road soon. Together, let's continue to celebrate the great music we love and keep it alive and rocking!

—Eddie Trunk, 2013

TOP: Lita Ford, Eddie, Ann Wilson, and Nancy Wilson
MIDDLE TOP: Eddie and photographer Ron Akiyama
MIDDLE BOTTOM: Eddie, Johnny Depp, Don Jamieson, and Jim Florentine
BOTTOM: Eddie and Jake E. Lee
LEFT: Eddie and Sammy Hagar

ACCEPT

When I think of the band Accept, the first thing that comes to mind are the riffs. Outside of Black Sabbath and maybe a few others, Accept—especially guitarist Wolf Hoffmann—is responsible for some of the catchiest and most brutally heavy guitar riffs in metal. These sonic assaults have formed the basis for some of the genre's best moments and laid the foundation for the speed metal movement that Accept helped pioneer. The band is one of Germany's greatest contributions to metal, and even though the band members are now all based in America, their sound retains a decidedly European feel: screaming, over-the-edge lead vocals, with menacing, chant-like backing vocals, and an anthemic, almost marching quality. Add in Hoffmann's brilliant, fast-tempo playing that incorporates classical influences, and you have all the hallmarks of classic Accept.

CLASSIC LINEUP:

PETER BALTES (BASS)

UDO DIRKSCHNEIDER (VOCALS)

HERMAN FRANK (GUITAR)

WOLF HOFFMANN (GUITAR)

STEFAN KAUFMANN (DRUMS)

KEY ADDITIONAL MEMBERS:

MICHAEL CARTELLONE (DRUMS)

JÖRG FISCHER (GUITAR)

DAVID REECE (VOCALS)

STEFAN SCHWARZMANN (DRUMS)

MARK TORNILLO (VOCALS)

DISCOGRAPHY

ABOVE: Mark Tornillo and Wolf Hoffmann

Accept's earliest history dates back to Germany in the late 1960s. However, the core lineup of Hoffmann, vocalist Udo Dirkschneider, and bassist Peter Baltes didn't truly come together until the mid-1970s. The band's self-titled debut album, released in 1979, went largely unnoticed in America. The follow-up was 1980's *I'm a Rebel*, whose title track became the band's first minor hit. The song was actually written for AC/DC by Alex Young, brother of Malcolm and Angus Young. When AC/DC passed on it, Accept grabbed it, understanding the anthemic potential of the song's spirit and message. The huge sing-along chorus became somewhat of a rallying cry for Accept's growing fan base. *I'm a Rebel* was a breakthrough for the band in Europe and put them on the map for the first time in the United States. The album also showed a band that was maturing, both as players and as writers, with progressively heavier and even more aggressive songs, as well as better production.

The following year's *Breaker* was another step forward, angrier and again even more forceful than *I'm a Rebel*. For proof of this, look no further than the track "Son of a Bitch." You can almost feel Accept screaming for attention from metal fans, demanding to be heard, and it all set the stage for what many feel to be one of the band's greatest works: 1982's *Restless and Wild*. By the time this album was released, Accept had been through the ups and downs of the business, done a great deal of touring, and fully developed their sound and image. Instead of worrying about radio play and commercial hits, they did what they do best: play huge, riff-based, uncompromising METAL. *Restless and Wild*'s first track, "Fast as a Shark," is often called one of the first-ever speed metal songs. It opens with the sound of a needle dropping on a crackling vinyl album and then moves to a very non-metal-sounding polka, before slowing down and slamming into Udo's scream of agony, a slashing guitar riff, and double-barrel bass drums. I always love when people hear "Fast as a Shark" for the first time. The look of horror on metal fans' faces during the first twenty seconds, before the song actually kicks in, is hysterical. Now, of course, this intro is such an iconic metal moment that fans often sing along with the "Hi-de, hi-do, hi-da" from the opening. With *Restless and Wild*, Accept made a defining metal statement. Metallica's first album had yet to come out, so the early roots of thrash can be traced back to this landmark album.

In 1983, Accept finally made their mark in America with the release of *Balls to the Wall*. It featured the best production yet on an Accept album—a bit slicker but still retaining their trademark heaviness. Like *Restless and Wild*, *Balls to the Wall* was produced by Dieter Dierks, who was known for his work with another legendary German heavy rock band, Scorpions. Dierks had helped Scorpions to finally crack America after more than a decade, and he helped Accept to do the same. While *Balls to the Wall*'s songs aren't as fast as some of the material on the previous album, they do feature some of Hoffmann's biggest and catchiest riffs. Finding a way to stay heavy but also be accessible is a tricky tightrope to walk for most metal bands, and Accept delivers that balance perfectly on *Balls to the*

Wall, an album that still sounds amazing today from a production stand-point. The album's title track is without question Accept's all-time biggest hit. The video was a regular on MTV, and anyone who has seen it can't forget the diminutive Udo growling into the camera in a camouflage out-fit and riding a wrecking ball at the clip's end. "Turn Me On" was another favorite from the album, and played often over the PA at the metal clubs I would hang out in. Accept was suddenly embraced on a large scale in America, which was finally ready for its heavy assault, and it led to tour-ing opportunities that included a bunch of dates supporting Kiss. I saw many of these shows, and I can tell you there were many nights that Ac-cept was a hard act to follow.

Metal Heart was released in 1985, and its title track also became an Ac-cept classic, that to this day is a set opener on many tours. Other songs from this album, like "Midnight Mover," got some serious airplay. How-ever, "Screaming for a Love-Bite" saw Accept drift into too-commercial territory for their denim-and-leather fan base. With 1986's *Russian Rou-lette* they tried to get back to a more aggressive sound, but it just wasn't clicking, and to many metal fans, Accept's moment was over. By now fans looking for heavier music were immersed in Metallica, Anthrax, and Megadeth, and Accept fell through the cracks.

In 1987 Udo announced he was leaving Accept to pursue a solo career. Oddly, the band endorsed his decision, perhaps thinking that a new Amer-ican singer would help win over U.S. fans again. Accept's first non-Udo album was 1989's *Eat the Heat*, with American David Reece on vocals. It simply did not work. Udo's gravelly voice was a huge part of the Ac-cept sound, and the new material wasn't the band's best. After their short tour with W.A.S.P., Reece was dismissed, and Accept drifted away from the scene completely. The band relaunched for a few years when Udo returned to the fold in 1993, but by then musical tastes in America were very much away from the metal scene, and the three new albums Accept made with their original singer were largely ignored and barely released in America. In the mid-2000s, though, the quality of metal that Accept had made at their height started to take on a new status with metal fans, and there seemed to be genuine demand for Accept. By now fans were missing Accept, so in 2005 the band launched again, with core members Dirkschneider, Baltes, and Hoffmann on board for a run of live dates at European festivals. Reviews were stellar, leading to what many thought would be a new Accept album and more extensive live shows. But un-fortunately that never happened. Udo stunned metal fans everywhere when he declined to continue working with Accept and instead chose to continue with his own group, U.D.O. Again, Accept fell back into obscurity.

It was in 2009 that I got a call from an old friend from New Jersey named Mark Tornillo, who was the singer for the legendary Jersey band T.T. Quick. The band had released a true underground classic on their own in 1986 called *Metal of Honor* but failed to break on a national level. I was an early supporter and had remained good friends with Mark over the years. He was now working as a union electrician and singing in some

UNDERGROUND CLASSIC

Wolf Hoffmann is one of rock's most underrated guitarists. Check out his instrumental album, *Clas-sical*. And to hear more from Mark Tornillo, the T.T. Quick album *Metal of Honor* is a must.

ACCEPT

1. BLOOD OF THE NATIONS
2. BALLS TO THE WALL
3. SON OF A BITCH
4. TURN ME ON
5. STALINGRAD

6. RESTLESS AND WILD
7. FAST AS A SHARK
8. METAL HEART
9. I'M A REBEL
10. MIDNIGHT MOVER

TOP: Udo Dirkschneider and Wolf Hoffmann
BOTTOM: Peter Baltes and Wolf Hoffmann
OPPOSITE LEFT: Mark Tornillo and Wolf Hoffmann
OPPOSITE TOP RIGHT: Peter Baltes, Eddie, and Wolf Hoffmann
OPPOSITE BOTTOM RIGHT: Udo Dirkschneider and Eddie

cover bands on the Jersey club scene for fun. Mark told me he had recently been contacted to go and jam with Peter and Wolf from Accept, who were now based in America and hoping to give the band another go without their iconic lead singer, who still refused to participate. I was truly excited for Mark, who is a great guy and a talented musician, with a vocal quality that was perfect for Accept. Weeks later, Mark came by my house, popped in a CD, and asked me to have a listen. It was him, with Accept, singing not only Udo's material but also killer brand-new music! I was blown away. I had to keep quiet about everything for a bit, but Mark assured me that I would be in on the ground floor and be able to break the news on the band, play their new music first, and present their first-ever live show. Things moved quickly, and true to their word, on May 8, 2010, I had the honor of introducing Accept for their first live show at a sold-out Gramercy Theatre in New York City with my old friend Mark Tornillo on vocals. Some fans were skeptical of Accept trying again without Udo, and with an American singer, but all were silenced by what went down that night. The band attacked the stage with a newfound energy and swagger. Mark gave his all to the classics and the gravel-throated growls and screams that many wondered if Udo could even muster any longer.

The icing on the cake that truly solidified this new union was the band's first album with Mark on board. *Blood of the Nations* was released in September 2010 and is a modern-day metal masterpiece. For the first time since *Balls to the Wall*, Wolf's riffs are on par with the band's classic moments, and Mark's vocals and writing are a perfect blend. We named *Blood of the Nations* "album of the year" on *That Metal Show*. It was that great. Worldwide touring ensued, and Accept's European fans, at first skeptical of an American being in the band, were also won over. I was so proud of my friend Mark, who was finally getting the recognition he deserved as a singer and writer. He overnight went from working a day job to fronting Accept and opening stadium shows for AC/DC (two bands he once performed covers of in the early days of T.T. Quick!). In 2012, Accept issued its second album with Mark, titled *Stalingrad*, which received even more international acclaim. I am very happy to say Accept is truly back!

? DID YOU KNOW

Many of Accept's lyrics were written by the band's manager and Wolf Hoffmann's wife, Gaby, under the name Deaffy. She had the best grasp of English in the early days.

In addition to playing in Accept, Hoffmann also works as a commercial photographer.

Legendary record producer Michael Wagener was a part of the very early history of Accept, first playing in the band and later working on some of their albums.

ALICE IN CHAINS

Back in the late '80s, while working for Megaforce Records, I would attend an annual event in Los Angeles called Foundations Forum. It was a music industry conference that was targeted toward the rock and metal crowd. Most label people would congregate at the hotel, attend panels with various Q&As, and show off their upcoming releases to others in the industry. There were also performances by both established and up-and-coming bands. So there was a heavy influx of A&R people looking for the next great band or telling others about a great new band they had signed. In 1989 I was on the conference's A&R panel with, among other reps, a guy by the name of Nick Terzo. Nick and I would talk from time to time about unsigned bands and who we liked or didn't. I always approached A&R work as not only seeing and listening to new bands but also connecting with others who I respected in the business to share thoughts. It's a competitive part of the industry, but I viewed this sort of feedback as useful, and it helped me to get a feel for what others were seeing and hearing.

CLASSIC LINEUP:

JERRY CANTRELL (GUITAR/VOCALS)

SEAN KINNEY (DRUMS)

LAYNE STALEY (VOCALS)

MIKE STARR (BASS)

KEY ADDITIONAL MEMBERS:

WILLIAM DUVALL (VOCALS)

MIKE INEZ (BASS)

OPPOSITE: Mike Starr and Layne Staley

DISCOGRAPHY

RIGHT (clockwise): Layne Staley, Mike Starr, Jerry Cantrell, and Sean Kinney
ABOVE: Jerry Cantrell
OPPOSITE: Layne Staley

Prior to our panel, Nick and I met with the rest of the group speaking that day. Everyone was talking about a band Nick had just signed called Alice in Chains. I remember countless people asking, "How are things with Alice?" Or saying, "Alice could be huge!" My initial thought was that he had signed Alice Cooper! But I then learned that Alice in Chains was a new band from Seattle—though I had never heard of them, the buzz at the industry gathering was everywhere, so it didn't surprise me when they made a huge mark on the scene soon after.

In addition to working at the label, I was also doing my weekend metal radio show. About a year after first hearing of Alice in Chains, I was sent an EP with a song called "We Die Young." It was my first listen to the band, and I was stunned by how heavy and haunting it was. Alice in Chains was very much a metal band back then, and they were marketed and sold that way. (The term "grunge" hadn't been universally branded yet.) But along with the metal qualities—massive riffs, huge production, and dark lyrical themes—Alice in Chains also had a different quality about them. At times they could sound oddly uplifting. I know that sounds crazy, but I've always felt that way about their music. It could have a dark, depressing quality but also a certain brightness. I think much of this was due to the incredible vocals in the band. Lead singer Layne Staley had a voice that could scare you with its intensity, but when blended with guitarist Jerry Cantrell's vocals, it could have a totally different, layered effect. The band used the dual-lead-vocal approach many times in their music, and it really was one of the qualities that set them apart from others at the time.

"We Die Young" was one of the tracks included on the band's 1990 full-length debut, *Facelift*. I immediately embraced the album on my radio show and could hear why there had been so much excitement at the convention a year earlier. The big bands from the '80s were still doing well touring and getting play on MTV, but little did they know that the writing was on the wall with Alice in Chains and the other emerging Seattle bands that would radically shift the world of music. Jani Lane from Warrant, a band that shared a label with Alice in Chains, once told a story of the day he walked into Columbia Records and the poster for his band's latest album was being taken down from the lobby and replaced with an Alice in Chains poster. The writing was literally on the wall.

Some of the band's earliest touring was opening for other hard rock bands of the time, like Van Halen, Extreme, and even Poison. There were some obvious mismatches in fan bases, but Alice in Chains was still searching for the audience that would embrace them. They didn't have the obvious commercial hooks for the pop metal fans, they didn't have a flamboyant guitar hero, they didn't have a pinup-style frontman, but they did have stirring songs with memorable vocal melodies. Although nobody would question that the band was heavy, and perhaps even the most metal-sounding of the grunge movement, they were not fast in tempo—so the speed/thrash crowd didn't know what to make of them. But in 1991 Alice in Chains was the opening act on an arena tour known as Clash of the Titans that featured Anthrax, Megadeth, and Slayer. That's right, three of the most intense speed metal legends had a relatively unknown band as their opener! You see, the heavier bands of the day were drawn to the dark, plodding sound of *Facelift* and related more to Alice in Chains than to the glam metal bands of the day. Some nights Alice in Chains was well received, some nights the thrash-loving crowd didn't get it, but I truly feel this tour played a big part in the band's being more respected and loved by the metal community than the other grunge bands of that era.

Almost from day one, Alice in Chains was associated with drugs and substance abuse. This became very evident with the release of *Dirt*, their second full-length album. On *Dirt*, the band took a step forward into their deep, brooding sound and stark writing, much of it dealing with the struggles they were having with drugs. Most publicized was singer Layne Staley's use of heroin and cocaine. It's strange that *Dirt* is widely regarded as a masterpiece because of how introspective and raw some of its themes and songs are. As sick as it sounds, it probably could not have been the incredible album it is if the band hadn't been dealing with such personal battles. The band felt it was cleansing to put these personal issues into their songs, but it didn't help them kick their habits—as history would soon show. Even so, *Dirt* spawned huge songs like "Rooster," "Them Bones," and "Down in a Hole" and truly signaled the arrival of the grunge explosion that included Nirvana, Soundgarden, Pearl Jam, and a wave of soundalikes.

Alice in Chains went through their first lineup change when bassist Mike Starr left the band while they were touring as Ozzy Osbourne's opening act and was replaced by Mike Inez. But the band continued releasing extremely successful albums and EPs that were instantly embraced by radio

DID YOU KNOW **?**

One of the band's most popular albums is the EP *Jar of Flies*. This mostly acoustic collection was not recorded with the intent of being released.

EDDIE'S PLAYLIST

ALICE IN CHAINS

1. DAM THAT RIVER
2. WE DIE YOUNG
3. ANGRY CHAIR
4. CHECK MY BRAIN
5. HOLLOW

6. SEA OF SORROW
7. THEM BONES
8. DOWN IN A HOLE
9. ROOSTER
10. GRIND

TOP: William DuVall
BOTTOM: Mike Starr
OPPOSITE LEFT: William DuVall
and Jerry Cantrell
OPPOSITE RIGHT: Mike Inez

programmers (I cued their songs up countless times myself) and MTV into the mid-'90s. I found it ironic that many were kicking metal bands to the curb in favor of new, cooler bands like Alice in Chains, who just a couple of years earlier were being marketed in the same metal scene.

Rumors of Layne Staley's struggles continued to make the rounds, and when the band didn't tour in support of their 1995 self-titled release, it was a real sign that he was in serious trouble. The band performed at an *MTV Unplugged* show in early 1996, and later that year I saw one of their last appearances ever, when they opened the Kiss reunion tour at Tiger Stadium in Detroit. The band was OK at that time, but it was obvious that Layne was not doing well. He seemed to be holding on to the mic stand to stay upright, and his voice was thin and frail, making him lean more on Cantrell to fill out their signature vocal sound. They also did something that day that was not very wise—playing some classic Kiss riffs in between their own songs. I'm sure they saw it as a tribute, but the rabid Kiss fans waiting for this debut reunion performance interpreted it as mocking and disrespectful, and some in the audience booed. A few weeks later, Alice in Chains essentially ended, as they couldn't continue as they were. Although they never officially broke up, they all went their own ways, I assume, in hopes that Staley would get the help he needed. Over the next few years, Staley and Cantrell surfaced from time to time

Jerry Cantrell released two solo albums: 1998's *Boggy Depot* and 2002's *Degradation Trip*—which features current Metallica bassist Robert Trujillo and a guest appearance from Chris DeGarmo of Queensrÿche. Cantrell has also guested on albums by Circus of Power, Danzig, Metallica, and Richie Kotzen, among others.

The final studio recordings from Alice in Chains with Layne Staley came in the form of songs called "Died" and "Get Born Again," included as new material on the band's 1999 box set *Music Bank*.

for side and solo projects, but there was no Alice in Chains activity. The status of Layne's drug addiction was always being whispered about in rock circles, and it sadly came as no surprise that he was found dead in April of 2002 in his condo.

Even though many believed that seeing a version of the band live again also died that day, the surviving members turned up to jam at a few different charity events, with different guest singers for a song or two. One of those singers was a guy by the name of William DuVall, who had been fronting a band called Comes with the Fall. DuVall's voice blended perfectly with Jerry's, and it was almost scary how much it sounded like Layne's. A highly successful tour took place in 2006 that set the stage for the 2009 release of a new Alice in Chains album titled *Black Gives Way to Blue*. It was a huge success, leading up to the release of a second new studio album in 2013. But the band's drug issues also took down former member Mike Starr in 2011. Starr, who had appeared on the VH1 show *Celebrity Rehab*, continued to struggle with drugs. He was a huge Kiss fan and swore that if Ace Frehley came on the show to talk to him about getting sober, he would clean up. But even that didn't work, and sadly, Mike Starr passed away soon afterward.

ANGEL

n the 1970s, I was introduced to music and set on my path to rock obsession. In 1976 I purchased my first Kiss record, and from that point, it was on! I had to know everything about every rock band that came on the radio. As a preteen, my mentality was more about scouting any competition to the throne of Kiss than about actually appreciating new music. I needed to listen, watch, and research so that no band would pose a threat to my masked heroes. One group I heard a lot about back then was Angel. It seemed like almost every magazine I picked up had photos of this group and compared them to Kiss. Angel was on the same label as Kiss (Casablanca), and Gene Simmons had been an early champion of the band. But that's where the comparisons ended. Where Kiss was dark and evil, spitting blood and breathing fire, Angel was white and pretty and, well, angelic in their image. Their musical styles were different, too. Kiss had a meat-and-potatoes, basic hard rock guitar approach, while Angel's was progressive, with a more polished and melodic sound that included keyboards. Seeing the amount of press and marketing around Angel in the mid- to late '70s would have given anyone the impression they were a much bigger band than they ever were, but the hype was far greater than any sales they achieved.

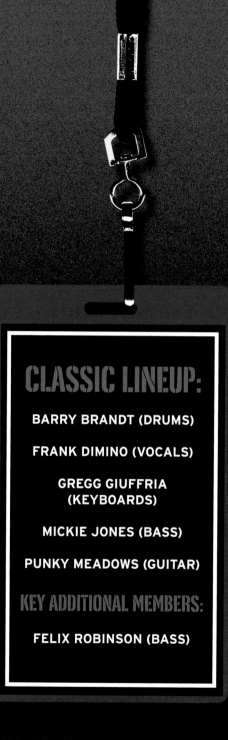

CLASSIC LINEUP:

BARRY BRANDT (DRUMS)

FRANK DIMINO (VOCALS)

GREGG GIUFFRIA (KEYBOARDS)

MICKIE JONES (BASS)

PUNKY MEADOWS (GUITAR)

KEY ADDITIONAL MEMBERS:

FELIX ROBINSON (BASS)

OPPOSITE: Punky Meadows, Frank Dimino, and Mickie Jones

DISCOGRAPHY

ANGEL (1975)

HELLUVA BAND (1976)

ON EARTH AS IT IS IN HEAVEN (1977)

WHITE HOT (1978)

SINFUL (1979)

LIVE WITHOUT A NET (1980)

IN THE BEGINNING (1999)

ABOVE: Punky Meadows
RIGHT: Punky Meadows and Frank Dimino
OPPOSITE TOP: Gregg Giuffria
OPPOSITE BOTTOM: Frank Dimino,
Don Jamieson, Eddie, Chris Kael (of Five
Finger Death Punch), and Jim Florentine

Angel first came together in the early '70s in Washington, D.C., where the original members played in various club bands. The first lineup consisted of vocalist Frank Dimino, keyboardist Gregg Giuffria, guitarist Punky Meadows, drummer Barry Brandt, and bassist Mickie Jones. In their earliest years, Angel was more of a harder-looking and -sounding band. Punky Meadows was an immediate star. Not only did he have a great name, but he also had a glam look, with long, flowing jet-black hair and pouting facial expressions. But Punky was not all flash—the guy could really play. He was a natural rock star who could fire off some tasty licks from the Strat slung low around his waist. Frank had a soaring voice that could reach the high notes but also tell a very convincing story in its delivery. And in Gregg, Angel had its mad scientist of keyboards—like a hard rock Keith Emerson with a touch of Jon Lord. Gregg would sometimes leave his massive keyboard rig and come out to the front of the stage wearing a keyboard like a guitar around his neck and rock with the band.

Angel's self-titled debut had some modest success and was fairly well reviewed. Much of the attention was given to the album's nearly seven-minute opening track, "The Tower"—to this day considered the band's finest, most epic moment. The song has an immediate conceptual feel to it, with its space-age sound effects and Dimino recounting some sort of futuristic tale before his voice goes soaring into the stratosphere. This leads into one of the band's signatures: the Meadows vs. Giuffria guitar/keyboard trade-off. Perhaps the most unique thing is how they masterfully merged their pop hooks to result in epic "pomp rock" (like arena rock) songs. The album is at times heavy with big, catchy riffs and at times melodic, establishing Angel's glam-meets-progressive-rock sound.

Like many '70s bands, Angel kept pumping out albums in hopes that one would stick and truly sell. *Helluva Band* and *On Earth as It Is in Heaven* showed some evolution toward a more mainstream hard rock approach without compromising the band's sound. But Angel moved into a glossier, pop metal direction in 1978 with *White Hot*, which scored them some minor hits. While the sales and radio play never really came for them, their marketing campaign exploded. It was almost as if Casablanca, which was having massive success with Kiss at the time, as well as many popular disco acts, was taking some of that money and throwing it at Angel. The band had adopted a look where they dressed in white satin jumpsuits. They also had a new logo that to this day is one of the coolest I've ever seen: an ambigram that read "Angel" upside down and right-side up.

The stage show got bigger and bigger, too. At some shows the band was introduced by a holographic talking sphinx, with each member appearing to materialize out of thin air when his name was called—an illusion developed by magician Doug Henning. At one point, the members even emerged from pods on the stage surrounded by smoke. Sound a bit like the classic scene in the film *This Is Spinal Tap*? Well, rumor has it, that's exactly where the filmmakers got the idea! Angel drummer Barry Brandt was scared of getting stuck in the pod and often stood next to it, refusing to actually go inside. At the peak of the Angel stage show, the band members would ascend into their own exploding logo! Their live show carried them to the point of headlining theaters, but they never upgraded to an arena level. They also couldn't get in front of other bands' audiences. (For example, they shared a label with Kiss, but Kiss would never share a bill with them.) And as an opening act, Angel had live tricks that were hard

ANGEL

1. GOT LOVE IF YOU WANT IT
2. WHITE LIGHTNING
3. OVER AND OVER
4. THE WINTER SONG
5. THE FORTUNE
6. DON'T LEAVE ME LONELY
7. CAN YOU FEEL IT
8. ROCK & ROLLERS
9. FEELIN' RIGHT
10. THE TOWER

to compete with, so other headliners weren't interested. One of my great regrets is that I never experienced these live shows firsthand—by 1980, when I was finally old enough to take in a live show, Angel was done.

Angel never got a big hit single and their album sales were stagnant, so Casablanca could no longer fund them and the band broke up. I think their music fell between the cracks in some ways, because it was too progressive for commercial airplay and not hard enough to win over the metal fan base. Ironically, the end came just when it seemed that Angel was about to get a break. A B-side from *White Hot* called "The Winter Song" started to get airplay around the holidays, and the band quickly retitled it "The Christmas Song" to capitalize on seasonal radio. And Angel also appeared in the Jodie Foster film *Foxes*, about teens growing up in Los Angeles. Casablanca produced the film and cast Angel as the rock band the kids were going to see in concert. It features some brief but rare live concert footage. I say "rare" because, shockingly, Angel's extremely visual live show had never been filmed. Like their labelmates Kiss, who five years earlier were about to break up but finally exploded because of the strength of a live album, Angel's final release with the original lineup (and last shot at success) was the double album *Live Without a Net*. Although it captures some of the live energy of the band's

show, it still couldn't save Angel. I often have wondered if a band as visual as Angel might have been saved by a TV channel that was about to emerge: MTV.

As I've often said, Angel was a band that people either loved or never heard of, and therefore they have achieved cult status. So in the late '90s, there was a reunion (along with an album, *In the Beginning*, by the new lineup), providing the only time I would see a version of Angel live. This lineup included only Frank and Barry from the original band, and without the much-loved Punky Meadows, interest was minimal at best. They were also unable to revive their infamous live show—without any real financial backing, they couldn't bring out any of their old stage tricks. Although Frank could still deliver the songs, it just wasn't the Angel reunion that it could have been. (And if Angel didn't make it big years ago, how much audience could there be?) A few years ago, I was in Las Vegas on vacation seeing a local band called the Sin City Sinners. It was a great surprise when the band welcomed Frank Dimino to the stage to play some Angel classics. Frank, who now lives in Vegas, could still belt them out as well as he did in the '70s, and it was truly great to see. In 2012, Frank made a cameo appearance on *That Metal Show* and announced a new band he had formed with Oz Fox from Stryper called Vinyl Tattoo.

UNDERGROUND CLASSIC

In 2012 the British label Rock Candy Records released deluxe, remastered editions of the first three Angel albums, which had been very hard to find on CD.

ABOVE: Frank Dimino, Gregg Giuffria, and Mickie Jones
OPPOSITE: Frank Dimino

BLUE ÖYSTER CULT

Despite having their songs covered by a diverse list of rock and metal artists like Sebastian Bach, Metallica, Iced Earth, HIM, Racer X, and countless others, Blue Öyster Cult doesn't always get the credit they should for their impact as one of metal's earliest bands. The group's history dates back to Long Island, New York, in the late '60s, and they still continue to this day with remaining original members Eric Bloom and Donald "Buck Dharma" Roeser. Band manager, lyricist, and producer Sandy Pearlman played an important role in much of their early career, guiding and shaping BÖC's image, sound, and even their name. They were originally called Soft White Underbelly, until Pearlman suggested the change to Blue Öyster Cult, after a group of aliens in a poem he had written (remember, it was the '60s!).

CLASSIC LINEUP:

ERIC BLOOM
(VOCALS/GUITAR)

ALBERT BOUCHARD
(DRUMS/VOCALS)

JOE BOUCHARD
(BASS/VOCALS)

ALLEN LANIER
(GUITAR/KEYBOARDS)

**DONALD "BUCK DHARMA"
ROESER (GUITAR/VOCALS)**

KEY ADDITIONAL MEMBERS:

RICK DOWNEY (DRUMS)

DANNY MIRANDA (BASS)

JULES RADINO (DRUMS)

JON ROGERS (BASS)

**BOBBY RONDINELLI
(DRUMS)**

DISCOGRAPHY

ABOVE: Eric Bloom, Richie Castellano,
Buck Dharma, Kasim Sulton, and
Jules Radino (on drums)
OPPOSITE: Allen Lanier, Buck Dharma,
and Joe Bouchard

There was always such a sense of mystery around BÖC—the name, the strange song and album titles, the use of art on the album covers instead of photos of the band, the literary and sci-fi inspired lyrics (some even penned by Patti Smith and Jim Carroll)—that in the beginning it really seemed like they were a cult making some psychedelic metal. BÖC was also a different kind of band because the focus wasn't on a star lead singer or guitarist, but instead a dark and enigmatic (and at times trippy) vibe that ran through their music and album covers. There was a very early idea to take this even further and assign all the band members strange sci-fi-sounding names, but it was soon dropped. The only one who embraced and retained his alter ego name was guitarist Donald Roeser, who is equally OK with being called "Buck Dharma" to this day.

After some initial lineup changes and recordings for Elektra Records that were never released, the official launch of Blue Öyster Cult came with the band's self-titled debut on Columbia in 1972. Signed to the label by music industry mogul Clive Davis, BÖC was very much modeled as an American version of Black Sabbath, who had started in the U.K. around the same time and experienced great early success with their first few albums. It's important to remember that Sabbath are widely regarded as the founding fathers of metal, so it should be noted how unique it was for an American band to take a similar approach, with a dark sound and riff-based heavy rock, at such an early time in metal's history. BÖC came out on Sabbath's heels, and the influence was noticeable when I first discovered their music years later. For proof of BÖC's brand of doom rock, look no further than the debut album opener "Transmaniacon MC." Other titles include "Screams," "She's as Beautiful as a Foot," and the closest to a hit, "Cities on Flame with Rock and Roll" (reminiscent of Sabbath's "The Wizard"). Stare at the weird three-dimensional-looking cover, crank up this debut, imagine massive amounts of pot being smoked, and you are immediately transported back to 1972!

The band's original recording lineup remained intact for many years. Guitarists/vocalists Bloom and Roeser, along with guitarist Allen Lanier

EDDIE'S PLAYLIST

BLUE ÖYSTER CULT

1. E.T.I. (EXTRA TERRESTRIAL INTELLIGENCE)
2. HEAVY METAL: THE BLACK AND SILVER
3. R. U. READY 2 ROCK
4. JOAN CRAWFORD
5. ASTRONOMY
6. CITIES ON FLAME WITH ROCK AND ROLL
7. VETERAN OF THE PSYCHIC WARS
8. BURNIN' FOR YOU
9. TAKE ME AWAY
10. GODZILLA

ABOVE: Eric Bloom, Eddie, and Buck Dharma

(yes, BÖC had a three-guitar attack—always cool!) and brothers Joe (bass) and Albert (drums) Bouchard as the rhythm section, recorded all of the band's classic '70s albums, such as *Tyranny and Mutation*, *Secret Treaties*, *Agents of Fortune*, and *Spectres*. BÖC's fan base was built slowly and deliberately, mostly from their shows, where the music really came alive. I always thought many of the band's early albums suffered from a less-than-dynamic sound, but BÖC songs were perfect for the arena stages, where an often-impaired (i.e., high as a kite) audience could zone out to the heavy riffs, menacing sound, and intense lighting. This resulted in two classic live albums: 1975's *On Your Feet or on Your Knees* and the 1978 bestseller *Some Enchanted Evening* (the 2012 box set version contains live concert video footage from 1978).

My introduction to Blue Öyster Cult came while I was still in high school, almost ten years after they first formed. The same way I discovered much of the music I came to love—by randomly browsing through my local record store, seeing a cover I thought looked cool, and asking the clerk if it was any good—I grabbed 1981's *Fire of Unknown Origin* because of its haunting cover. With its depiction of unsettling occult-like aliens wearing strange hooded robes with symbols on them, I was sold! *Fire of Unknown Origin* saw BÖC at the height of their popularity. By then, they had scored some huge radio hits with "Don't Fear the Reaper" and "Godzilla," and

with *Fire* they had another massive single with "Burnin' for You." I also loved the song "Veteran of the Psychic Wars" and the ultra-creepy "Joan Crawford," with its terrifying chant: "Christina, Mommy's home!" It was powerful stuff for me in my teenage years that made a lasting impact.

Blue Öyster Cult featured prominently in an animated film called *Heavy Metal* that was all the rage in the early '80s. They also embarked on a now-legendary co-headlining tour with Black Sabbath that was filmed for a theatrical release called *Black and Blue*. A few years earlier, this probably would have been a stadium show, but Sabbath was on their first tour without Ozzy Osbourne and was introducing Ronnie James Dio, to a mixed reaction. Regardless, two bands that had gotten their start around the same time and were both based in dark grooves was a huge attraction. Sabbath and BÖC took turns closing the show and played sets of equal length. Dio told me much later that this was a rough tour for him. He was new to Sabbath and trying to win over a tough crowd. Dealing with the egos of two headlining bands and a ton of gear onstage made set changes even more stressful. But the *Black and Blue* tour has achieved great status with metal fans who saw it, or who saw the widely boot-legged concert film. The movie has never properly been released on DVD, which frustrates many. When I spoke with Eric and Buck about this in a

TOP LEFT: Eric Bloom and Allen Lanier
TOP RIGHT: Eric Bloom and Buck Dharma
BOTTOM RIGHT: Allen Lanier, Buck Dharma, and Joe Bouchard

Onetime BÖC drummer Rick Downey went on to become a lighting designer and tour manager for many bands. He was road manager for Anthrax, as well as others, during the late '80s.

Former Rainbow drummer Bobby Rondinelli also played in BÖC, as did legendary metal bassist Rudy Sarzo, who toured with them for a few years.

2012 interview, they explained that it was Tony Iommi who didn't want it released. Apparently Tony and Sabbath weren't happy with their performance the night it was shot—also a night that Sabbath opened the show.

As the mid-'80s rolled around, BÖC suffered the same fate as many bands from the '70s who were trying to fit in with the MTV era. Never a very visual band in person, they did their best to adapt and play a more radio-friendly musical style and did score some popular music videos. But their sound also began to get a bit too polished and commercial for serious BÖC fans. *Club Ninja*, released in 1986, features many outside songwriters, and the first major lineup change took place with Albert Bouchard leaving over various differences with his bandmates. But through many lineup changes and various trends in music, Blue Öyster Cult has never stopped touring. They made their name this way, and to this day, they still play shows on a consistent basis. I interviewed the band for TV for the first time in 2005 at the Sturgis Bike Rally in South Dakota for VH1 Classic. Even then, BÖC was still a major draw, especially for that crowd. Eric and Buck are pretty laid-back guys, happy to play live, make the occasional new music, and enjoy the audience that turns up to hear their many classics. They also have a great sense of humor. As a matter of fact, when we started taping that TV special, Eric did the entire interview wearing fake, plastic bulging eyeballs!

I think Blue Öyster Cult sometimes gets left out of the conversation of important, groundbreaking metal bands because they were never 100 percent locked into the metal sound. Where Sabbath remained heavy from day one, Blue Öyster Cult incorporated long jams and psychedelic sounds in their music—they could sound like Santana or the Doors—and also experimented with progressive, and at times commercial, tracks. But it's important to remember that BÖC and metal were born around the same time, and BÖC chose to evolve over a forty-year period. Few bands have enjoyed this kind of longevity. Without question, Blue Öyster Cult was a pioneer of metal in sound and image, and songs like "Godzilla" and "Cities on Flame" can rock with the best of them. I challenge you to spend one day listening to classic rock radio without hearing "Burnin' for You" or "Don't Fear the Reaper"—truly timeless classics.

ABOVE: Eric Bloom and Buck Dharma
OPPOSITE LEFT: Buck Dharma
OPPOSITE RIGHT: Eric Bloom
and Albert Bouchard

BUCKCHERRY

Buckcherry formed at the height of Seattle's alternative rock movement, but the band had little to do with the sounds of 1995. Originally using the name Sparrow, they later became Buckcherry—borrowing the moniker from a drag queen they knew. I first became aware of the band when their 1999 self-titled debut (coproduced by legendary Sex Pistol Steve Jones) was released on DreamWorks Records, a relatively new label that legendary Hollywood director Steven Spielberg had a piece of. I was fairly disillusioned with the music that had been showing up in my mailbox at my radio station back then. It all sounded the same, with some connection to the Nirvana-led grunge movement. But Buckcherry was totally different. Their debut—a raw, in-your-face collection of songs with huge, buzzing dual guitars, great hooks, and a singer with a great voice and a punk rock attitude—was everything I loved about hard rock music. The album was recorded by the founding lineup: vocalist Josh Todd, guitarist Keith Nelson, bassist Jonathan Brightman, and drummer Devon Glenn; second guitarist Yogi came on board shortly after the debut was complete.

CLASSIC LINEUP:

JIMMY ASHURST (BASS)

STEVIE D. (GUITAR)

XAVIER MURIEL (DRUMS)

KEITH NELSON (GUITAR)

JOSH TODD (VOCALS)

KEY ADDITIONAL MEMBERS:

JONATHAN "J.B." BRIGHTMAN (BASS)

DEVON GLENN (DRUMS)

YOGI (GUITAR)

OPPOSITE: Jimmy Ashurst, Xavier Muriel, Stevie D., Josh Todd, Eddie, and Keith Nelson

DISCOGRAPHY

BUCKCHERRY (1999)

TIME BOMB (2001)

15 (2006)

BLACK BUTTERFLY (2008)

ALL NIGHT LONG (2010)

CONFESSIONS (2013)

After two years of touring in support of their debut, Buckcherry released the all-important second album. Second albums tell so much about a band's makeup and longevity. Most bands have their whole early career to struggle and write and get a deal for their first album, but often only a year or less to come up with material for a follow-up. *Time Bomb* was issued in 2001, and I was happy to hear it was more of the same—another ripping assault with even better production. There was a great feeling of urgency and edge in the recording, something many bands lose after having debut-album success while chasing a more commercial sound. "Frontside," "Ridin'," "Time Bomb," "Porno Star" (the parent of the band's "Crazy Bitch," in my view), and "Whiskey in the Morning" rock as hard as anything Buckcherry has ever done. But *Time Bomb* also has a Stones-sounding side as well, on songs like "Slit My Wrists" and "Helpless." To me, the album is as good as, if not better than, their debut. But for whatever reason, the album bombed. The group's hard-core fans loved it, but it seemed like most fans of the first album had written Buckcherry off, and therefore label support was not as strong.

When *Time Bomb* came out, which was around when Aerosmith released *Just Push Play,* I was doing some freelance music reviews in addition to my radio shows. I am a huge fan of Aerosmith, whose influence on Buckcherry is obvious, and while I was deeply disappointed in *Just Push Play*, I loved *Time Bomb*. I wrote a review of it for *Metal Edge* magazine and ended it by saying, "*Time Bomb* is the type of album Aerosmith wishes they were still making. Just push eject and buy this instead." Then I went to see Buckcherry play live at Irving Plaza in New York and attended the afterparty at a nearby bar. Even though *Time Bomb* didn't have a hit and didn't sell as well as their debut, the group still pulled a

great crowd of new and old rock fans. Their music lends itself to being played live and loud in a hot, sweaty club. Todd is also a great frontman who doesn't miss a note. I had never met the band before, but after that gig I introduced myself to Keith Nelson, and before I could even finish a word he said, "I know who you are, and I have the *Metal Edge* review you wrote for *Time Bomb* on my refrigerator at home!" Keith was appreciative of my support for the album and band, and we had a good talk that night and agreed to stay in touch. But less than a year later, I heard the news that Buckcherry was done. The disappointment of *Time Bomb*, along with some rising tensions and disagreements in the band, pushed them to call it quits in 2002.

How could it be that a band that had such great success out of the gate, even playing the Woodstock Festival, could be considered old news just a couple of years after releasing a gold debut? Even though Buckcherry had put out only two albums, the members of the group were not young by music business standards, as they had all been on the L.A. music scene for a while before getting a deal. But rarely is the music industry fair in any way, and I think everyone just wrote them off as one-hit wonders to some degree. After the band's breakup, Josh and Keith continued to work together in an early version of Velvet Revolver. And in 2004 Todd released a very heavy solo album called *You Made Me* on an independent label. I liked the album, and he seemed intent on moving forward as a solo artist and making more aggressive music. But *You Made Me* barely registered with the public, and the tour was poorly attended. I saw one of his shows, and most fans were disappointed in the change of direction and the fact that Todd did only a couple of Buckcherry songs live, with new arrangements.

LEFT: Keith Nelson and Stevie D.
ABOVE: Jimmy Ashurst
OPPOSITE RIGHT: Keith Nelson and Josh Todd
OPPOSITE LEFT: Stevie D.

EDDIE'S PLAYLIST

BUCKCHERRY

1. WHISKEY IN THE MORNING
2. DEAD AGAIN
3. RESCUE ME
4. SUNSHINE
5. SO FAR

6. BROKEN GLASS
7. OUT OF LINE
8. FRONTSIDE
9. CRUSHED
10. RIDIN'

TOP: Keith Nelson
BOTTOM: Xavier Muriel
OPPOSITE LEFT: Josh Todd
OPPOSITE RIGHT: Eddie with
Buckcherry's platinum record

In 2005 I received a call from an old music industry friend who told me that he was now working in management and representing a reformed Buckcherry. He knew I was an early supporter, so he wanted my input. The band had a new lineup built around the core of Josh and Keith, along with new members Jimmy Ashurst on bass, Xavier Muriel on drums, and Stevie D. on guitar. The band didn't have a record deal and was taking a total do-it-yourself approach to things. Keith began sending me tracks from the studio as soon as they were complete, and I started playing them on the radio. The songs were good—*really* good. And I helped get the word out that this band was coming back strong. But few seemed to care. Eventually Buckcherry was able to score a contract for the album *15* in Japan, and not long after, their management decided to release the album independently on their own label, Eleven Seven, in 2006. I distinctly remember hearing that the first track was going to be an obscenity-filled anthem to wild sex called "Crazy Bitch" and thinking it would be a huge mistake. Sure, it had a cool groove, but in my view, it was far from the best song on the album. Plus, how could it ever be played on the radio with the edits needed to clean up the language? Well, I'm proud to say that I couldn't have been more wrong and that "Crazy Bitch" was an enormous comeback for the band! *15* would go on to score several more hits, including the ballad "Sorry," and Atlantic Records came in and scooped up the album and rereleased it. When nobody wanted to touch them, Buckcherry did it

themselves, and now they were back in the big leagues. As I write this, it's with great pride that I look up at the gold and platinum albums hanging on my wall for *15*, as well as a note from Keith saying, "Eddie, you were there first, thanks for believing." Not being a musician myself, what I cherish most is being able to help bands I love get great music to the masses.

Buckcherry followed up the massive success of *15* with *Black Butterfly* in 2008, *All Night Long* in 2010, and a concept-themed album called *Confessions* in 2013. None have had the smash success of *15*, and the band is now back on an independent label, but they have built a loyal fan base, especially for their killer live shows—they are the ultimate road dogs, almost constantly on tour somewhere in the world. We remain great friends to this day, and I have the utmost respect for their talent and resilience in what can be a very unforgiving business.

CINDERELLA

clearly remember the day an advance copy of an album by a new band called Cinderella arrived on my desk in 1986. I took one look at the album cover and wrote off the band as yet another in a series of groups of the time that were more style than substance. Here were four guys posing in spandex, with their hair sprayed high and signature pouts on their faces. This look, while still very popular, was getting old for me. But I was encouraged by the label to listen before judging (always a good rule—and one I should have remembered at the time), so I popped in the tape and was shocked to hear the heaviness of the album's opener, the title track "Night Songs." It was instantly obvious to me that I had misjudged this album by its cover. Cinderella came out blazing with a sound more in line with AC/DC's than that of the melodic glam bands of the time. They certainly looked like Poison, Warrant, and the others, but despite the band's appearance and name, their music had more balls and attitude, and a certain darkness in their riffs and lyrics set them apart.

CLASSIC LINEUP:

ERIC BRITTINGHAM (BASS)

FRED COURY (DRUMS)

TOM KEIFER (VOCALS/GUITAR)

JEFF LABAR (GUITAR)

OPPOSITE: Jeff LaBar, Tom Keifer, and Eric Brittingham

DISCOGRAPHY

Cinderella came from the Philadelphia area, where they gigged in the early '80s with lineups that included original members Tom Keifer on vocals and guitar and Eric Brittingham on bass. Guitarist Jeff LaBar joined right before the recording of the debut album, and drummer Fred Coury came on board just in time to make the album's photo session. The band was brought to the attention of PolyGram Records by Jon Bon Jovi, who was recording in Philly and happened to see them perform at a local club. Impressed by their sound, Jon told his A&R rep, PolyGram's Derek Shulman, to come down and have a look, and the band was signed soon after. Jon Bon Jovi played another role in helping Cinderella get noticed—by singing backing vocals on a couple of *Night Songs* tracks and making a cameo in the video for another, "Somebody Save Me," along with Richie Sambora. It's hard to imagine now that Jon Bon Jovi was such a cheerleader for bands like Cinderella and Skid Row, since he has masterfully distanced himself from that scene today. Although Cinderella certainly got an assist from such a major rock star, the band had the goods to back it all up—unlike many of the other slick and styled bands of the era. *Night Songs* went on to triple-platinum status, and seemingly overnight the band's videos played in heavy rotation on MTV. The songs "Shake Me" and "Nobody's Fool" were radio staples, and soon fans were clamoring to see the band live.

Cinderella worked *Night Songs* hard, touring with Poison and other notables. In 1988 they released *Long Cold Winter*, which took a step in a more bluesy, rootsy direction—evident right at the start with "Bad Seamstress Blues," which slams into the hard rock of "Fallin' Apart at the Seams." "Gypsy Road," "The Last Mile," "Coming Home," and the essential power ballad "Don't Know What You Got (Till It's Gone)" all became fixtures on radio and TV. *Long Cold Winter* hit number 10 on the Billboard charts, and to this day the album remains a fan favorite.

Two years later, the band released *Heartbreak Station*, on which

ABOVE: Tom Keifer
**RIGHT: Fred Coury, Eric Brittingham,
Tom Keifer, and Jeff LaBar**

they refined their more bluesy, hard rock look and direction. Cinderella was evolving quickly into a comfortable Rolling Stones-meets-Lynyrd Skynyrd-meets-Aerosmith territory–a gutsy move when you consider that glam was still very much the order of the day. Yet somehow this new direction did not alienate their fan base. The title track and "Shelter Me" were big hits for Cinderella, even though *Heartbreak Station* wasn't as huge as the previous two albums.

As successful as Cinderella was, their reign was relatively short-lived. Shortly after the *Heartbreak Station* tour, drummer Fred Coury left the band to team up with Ratt singer Stephen Pearcy in a new group called Arcade. It was also at this time that Tom Keifer developed the first of many debilitating issues with his voice, including cysts and a hemorrhage of his vocal cords. He underwent several surgeries in an effort to get his voice back. As a result, the band's fourth (and to this day final) studio album, *Still Climbing*, wasn't released until 1994, with session drummer Kenny Aronoff providing the drum tracks. But by then, for right or wrong,

LEFT: Eric Brittingham, Tom Keifer, and Jeff LaBar

ABOVE: Jeff LaBar
RIGHT: Fred Coury
OPPOSITE LEFT: Tom Keifer
OPPOSITE RIGHT TOP: Fred Coury and Eddie
OPPOSITE RIGHT BOTTOM: Tom Keifer and Eddie

Cinderella had been put in the "Hair Bands of the '80s" category, and like most of those bands, they couldn't get arrested in the '90s!

Cinderella remained largely inactive for much of the next fifteen years. Live shows were attempted but often postponed or canceled because of Tom's ongoing issues with his voice. Many think these problems are a by-product of how he sings, using his upper register, but he has told me on many occasions that his singing technique is not the problem. He sings in his natural voice, but years of not warming up and cooling down properly have taken their toll on his vocal cords. While he's a perfectionist in many ways, he just didn't take care of his instrument like he needed to. It was frustrating for the band and their fans when in the late 2000s Cinderella would announce shows and then have to cancel them. Tom's voice was on the mend after more corrective procedures, but he didn't want to take the stage and tackle the ambitious vocals of his biggest hits without being confident that his pipes were fully there. But by 2010, though, Cinderella was once again an active touring band. The absence had created a greater demand for them than for most of their contemporaries.

With no disrespect to the other three members, all of whom play vital roles in the signature sound and live performances, Cinderella is and has always been Tom Keifer's band. Tom is the lead guitarist, keyboardist, and principal songwriter, and his raspy vocals are what make the band distinct. He's truly one of the best singers from the time—a cross between Janis Joplin and Steven Tyler (who has certainly been an influence in the performing department as well).

I've seen Cinderella countless times in the past few years, and it's staggering how good they sound now. Keifer's voice is so powerful onstage

that people have even called my radio show claiming that he wasn't singing live but instead had a vocal track running behind him. The band caught wind of this and found it funny and flattering at the same time. So they invited me to stand on the side of the stage at a gig and see for myself that there were no tapes running, which I did. I can confirm that what people hear live from Cinderella is truly legit, and a testament to the hard work they have put into returning to this high level of performance.

Many fans have asked me about the possibility of new music from Cinderella, as it's been nearly twenty years since their last album. In 2013, Tom Keifer released his first ever solo album, *The Way Life Goes*, and even performed some live shows in support of it with a new band. The album has many moments that sound like Cinderella, but at other times he stretches beyond the world of hard rock and touches on acoustic, blues, and even country. Releasing new music may have turned around Tom's thinking about a new Cinderella album as well. In an interview I conducted with him for *The Way Life Goes*, he said he wouldn't rule out going into the studio with his Cinderella bandmates once again.

DOKKEN

The story of Dokken is truly one of great dysfunction between the band's lead singer and founding member, Don Dokken, and the band's brilliant lead guitarist, George Lynch. The inability of the two to coexist in a band has robbed hard rock fans of what could have been so much more. Dokken's roots go all the way back to the mid-'70s, but the band didn't truly make a name for itself until the early '80s. The real break for Don Dokken came when he was flown to Germany in 1981 to assist with vocals for the Scorpions album *Blackout*. Scorpions lead singer Klaus Meine was recovering from surgery to correct damage to his vocal cords, so Don was enlisted by the album's producer to record vocals that the band could play along to until Klaus was ready to return. While there, Don got a German record deal for Dokken, which resulted in him getting picked up for a deal in the United States. The band's 1983 debut on Elektra, *Breaking the Chains*, was recorded with a lineup that featured Dokken, Lynch, drummer Mick Brown, and bassist Juan Croucier. However, after the album was complete, Croucier left Dokken to join Ratt and was replaced by Jeff Pilson.

CLASSIC LINEUP:

MICK BROWN (DRUMS)

DON DOKKEN (VOCALS)

GEORGE LYNCH (GUITAR)

JEFF PILSON (BASS)

KEY ADDITIONAL MEMBERS:

REB BEACH (GUITAR)

JUAN CROUCIER (BASS)

JON LEVIN (GUITAR)

SEAN MCNABB (BASS)

JOHN NORUM (GUITAR)

BARRY SPARKS (BASS)

DISCOGRAPHY

Breaking the Chains was better received in Europe, where the band was embraced by the press, than in the United States. Still, it got some people in America talking about this melodic hard rock band and its shredding lead guitarist. Those were Dokken's two signatures: Don was all about melody (not the multi-octave screams of the metal world) and George was just a beast on guitar. George looked great and played with a fire and an attack similar to that of Eddie Van Halen and other greats of the time. George, who had been in consideration for the guitarist gig in Ozzy's band, also wrote some killer music with Don. His ferocious style coupled with Don's sense of song structure made for a lethal combination that truly came together on the band's second album, *Tooth and Nail*. Tracks like "Into the Fire" and the power ballad "Alone Again" quickly found their way in heavy rotation on MTV, and Dokken soon began selling boatloads of albums, getting tons of radio play, and being booked on some of the biggest tours.

Under Lock and Key followed in '85, with even bigger hits like "In My Dreams" and "It's Not Love." In 1987, Dokken released the lead song for the hit film *A Nightmare on Elm Street 3*, called "Dream Warriors." (The video even features the band battling Freddy Krueger and rescuing actress Patricia Arquette!) In 1988, the band took part in a U.S. stadium tour called Monsters of Rock, sharing the stage with Van Halen, Scorpions, and Metallica. Thanks to their brand of hard rock, which had melody and looks for the girls and shredding guitar for the guys, Dokken was one of the biggest stories of the '80s. But that same year, the classic Dokken was done.

Almost from the beginning, there was infighting between Don and George. The two simply did not get along. Much of the press and attention over Dokken centered on Lynch, who, as mentioned, was a great player and performer. All the attention going to a guy named Lynch (who could sometimes be outspoken and unfiltered) was bound to bruise some egos in a band named after its lead singer. In Don's mind, it was his band and he ran it, but he knew that George was vital to the look, the sound, and record sales. Jeff Pilson and Mick Brown certainly contributed greatly—Jeff as a singer, player, and writer, and Mick (rightfully known as "Wild Mick" for his animated personality on and off the stage) behind his kit. But the intense dynamic between guitarist and singer was the core of the band's appeal, and the tension between the two led to its premature implosion. Often the sniping between Lynch and Dokken spilled out into the press, which ate it up. Rarely had people witnessed a group that was openly having major personality issues in its lineup. Both Don and George told me years later that their record label actually encouraged and embellished some of this fighting at the time, thinking it was another way to get people talking about the band. But I truly think it just comes down to

In addition to Ratt bassist Juan Croucier being a member of an early Dokken lineup, Ratt drummer Bobby Blotzer was also in Dokken in the late '70s. Ratt guitarist Warren DeMartini also had a stint in Dokken in the early '90s before joining Whitesnake for a tour.

In the '90s, George Lynch became immersed in the world of bodybuilding. He became so muscular that it impacted his dexterity and playing.

In 2012, Mick Brown was charged with a DUI for driving a golf cart while intoxicated.

while, joined Dio and worked with Michael Schenker. In the aftermath of Dokken, it seemed like Lynch Mob was the offshoot more embraced by fans: It had the band's fiery guitarist, and its music was more in the classic Dokken style than was Don's solo record, which didn't quite have the same approach and was a bit more modern. Neither came close to the success of their former band, and many wondered if the original band would give it one more try. Even though George and Don clearly had issues, there still seemed to be a mutual respect musically, based in the reality that they were stronger together than apart.

The original Dokken lineup did reunite in 1994. Don had written a new solo album to be called *Dysfunctional*, but he was persuaded by his label to make it a Dokken album and to bring back Lynch. As a result, the rerecorded *Dysfunctional* (never was an album more perfectly titled) ended up being a Dokken reunion record and finally hit stores in 1995. Although fans were clearly excited to have Dokken back together, response to the album was lukewarm. It was a different time for music, and the songs just didn't capture the spirit of the band's earlier work or have the same hooks. Soon, more of the old disagreements began again. Dokken managed to release *Shadowlife* in 1997, but it failed to garner any real interest. So, with the musical climate against them, and the two key members once again at each other's throats, the original Dokken was done once again.

Don, however, was not done with the band that bore his name. He continued Dokken with a revolving cast of musicians over the years. Most recently, the guitar slot has been held by Jon Levin, who is also Don's attorney. George has often told me that Levin is better at playing his old solos at times than he is! George, meanwhile, continues with Lynch Mob, which has had several lineups, and has released several solo albums. Jeff Pilson plays in Foreigner, while Mick Brown plays with Dokken, Lynch Mob,

ABOVE: Mick Brown
OPPOSITE: Don Dokken

EDDIE'S PLAYLIST

DOKKEN

1. WHEN HEAVEN COMES DOWN
2. TURN ON THE ACTION
3. TOOTH AND NAIL
4. IT'S NOT LOVE
5. THE HUNTER
6. BREAKING THE CHAINS
7. UNCHAIN THE NIGHT
8. KISS OF DEATH
9. INTO THE FIRE
10. IN MY DREAMS

TOP: George Lynch
BOTTOM: George Lynch, Jeff Pilson,
Eddie, and Mick Brown
OPPOSITE: George Lynch, Don Dokken,
Mick Brown, and Jeff Pilson

and Ted Nugent. In the countless interviews I have done over the years with all of the band's members, talk of a possible reunion would always come up. Would the third time be the charm?

In 2010, while booking a season of guests for *That Metal Show*, I decided I'd take a shot and see if I could talk both George and Don into coming on my show together and working out decades of ill will. There had been rumblings behind the scenes that they wanted to give it another go. They were scheduled to come on *TMS* and planned to announce to the world a third reunion. But as the taping date got closer, issues arose between them. In the end, they agreed to still come on the show together but could not announce a reunion, since Jeff had commitments with Foreigner and had yet to tell that band about any other plans. The result was a rather strange interview where they addressed some of their history and their *intention* to reunite soon. There was clearly some tension in the room, and at one point I joked that I felt like they could be breaking up before they had even reunited! George and Don assured everyone they were going to give it one last go with the original band, but Pilson had no intention of leaving Foreigner—he would just take a break from them when time would allow him to work with Dokken. It was clear Don and George were already not on the same page during the shoot that day and each had a different vision for working together. Sure enough, a few months

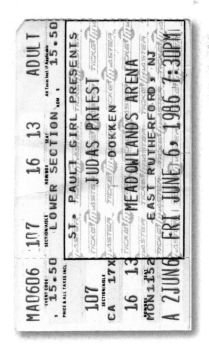
later, after coming on national TV and announcing a reunion (sort of), Lynch posted an apology on his Facebook page to me and all Dokken fans, saying that the reunion wasn't happening and that he simply couldn't work with Don. A year later, Lynch came back on *That Metal Show* with all the original Dokken members except Don and introduced another new band called T&N. Originally to be called Tooth and Nail (after the second Dokken album) but shortened for legal reasons, T&N plays Dokken songs and originals with three-quarters of the original lineup; in Don's version of Dokken, he's the sole original member. When I asked Lynch during the T&N interview why the reunion that had been mentioned on *That Metal Show* did not go forward, he claimed that Don wanted all the money. Shortly after that, Don came on my radio show and said that all of George's projects were not going anywhere and that he was just too difficult to work with. Dysfunctional indeed.

I truly like both Don and George, and all the other guys in Dokken for that matter. But the dynamic between Don and George is impossible to figure out and at times really fascinating. I have tried to give both of them platforms when they feel like talking, and I find them each to be honest and transparent. I have watched both the current Dokken and Lynch Mob play the same festivals and have seen Don and George embrace and talk backstage, then minutes later bad-mouth each other in interviews. At a festival in Oklahoma, I saw George watching Dokken's set. As I waited to intro Lynch Mob at the festival, George pondered whether it would be a good idea for him to play the same exact songs Dokken had just done. After all, they were his songs, too. But George ended up taking the high road and played mostly Lynch Mob tunes, with a few Dokken classics mixed in for good measure. In my recent conversation with Don in late 2012, he revealed to me he was retiring from making new music with Dokken and planning to explore collaborations with new artists and bands.

DREAM THEATER

The first time a publicist called me about having a member of Dream Theater on my radio show, he wanted to send the drummer. The drummer? Who ever talks to the drummer? Get me the main guy! Considering that drummer Mike Portnoy is a good friend now, and was one of the main guys, it's a funny thing for me to think back on. In all honesty, I do not live and breathe every song in the Dream Theater catalog. I do, however, have a massive respect for the band as musicians, as well as for the fan base they have built without compromising their vision. Few bands have fans as loyal and rabid as Dream Theater does, and few bands are as talented. Some of the stuff is a little out there and progressive leaning for my tastes, but they have some songs I truly love, and I'm one of the few who play their music on the radio. It's a major misconception that Dream Theater is all about musicianship and not songwriting. Just listen to tracks like "I Walk Beside You," "Forsaken," and "Wither." If there were any justice, these would have been hits. But with the fan base these guys have amassed, I don't think Dream Theater cares.

CLASSIC LINEUP:

JAMES LABRIE (VOCALS)

JOHN MYUNG (BASS)

JOHN PETRUCCI (GUITAR)

MIKE PORTNOY (DRUMS)

JORDAN RUDESS (KEYBOARDS)

KEY ADDITIONAL MEMBERS:

CHARLIE DOMINICI (VOCALS)

MIKE MANGINI (DRUMS)

KEVIN MOORE (KEYBOARDS)

DEREK SHERINIAN (KEYBOARDS)

OPPOSITE: Mike Portnoy, James LaBrie, John Petrucci, John Myung, and Jordan Rudess

DISCOGRAPHY

*WHEN DREAM
AND DAY UNITE* (1989)

IMAGES AND WORDS (1992)

AWAKE (1994)

FALLING INTO INFINITY
(1997)

*METROPOLIS PART 2:
SCENES FROM A MEMORY*
(1999)

*SIX DEGREES OF
INNER TURBULENCE* (2002)

TRAIN OF THOUGHT (2003)

OCTAVARIUM (2005)

SYSTEMATIC CHAOS (2007)

*BLACK CLOUDS AND
SILVER LININGS* (2009)

*A DRAMATIC
TURN OF EVENTS* (2011)

ABOVE: Mike Portnoy, John Myung,
James LaBrie, Kevin Moore, and John
Petrucci
RIGHT: Mike Portnoy

Dream Theater was formed under the original name Majesty in 1985 at Boston's Berklee College of Music by drummer Mike Portnoy, bassist John Myung, and guitarist John Petrucci—all technically accomplished and serious players (who have each topped numerous "best of" lists, including Portnoy's induction into the Modern Drummer Hall of Fame). The band members shared the same musical influences and the idea to assemble a committed group of skilled players who made music that truly takes you on a journey. The three-minute hit song is not what DT is all about. (I once played an entire 45-minute Dream Theater song to end my radio show. I had just under an hour's ride from Manhattan to my New Jersey home, and "Six Degrees of Inner Turbulence" played my entire ride back.)

Influenced by progressive and hard rock bands such as Pink Floyd, Rush, and Deep Purple, Dream Theater found a way to merge hard rock and heavy metal styles with ambitious concept albums and songs. The band signed to a small imprint of MCA called Mechanic Records and released their debut album, *When Dream and Day Unite*, in 1989, joined by vocalist Charlie Dominici and keyboardist Kevin Moore. But it wasn't until 1991 that the band's sound really began to take form. This was due not only to the arrival of new Canadian singer James LaBrie but also to the maturing of the band's direction and musicianship.

A major-label deal followed, and the release of 1992's *Images and Words* saw the band take a huge leap forward in writing, playing, and production. The album contains the track "Pull Me Under," which to this day is the closest they have ever come to a bona fide hit single—something the band pokes fun at with the title of their later compilation *Greatest Hit (. . . and 21 Other Pretty Cool Songs)*. *Images and Words* eventually went gold, and more important, cemented an incredibly passionate relationship with a growing number of fans who loved the band's unique precision and dedication to their craft. In the late '80s and early '90s, when so much of what was happening in music was about style over substance, Dream Theater built a fan base that cared about the complete opposite. And that base has seemed to grow on a global level with each album and

tour. It's an amazing luxury that so few bands enjoy: Regardless of radio or video play, press, TV appearances, or anything else, they know they are always going to sell albums and play to full venues. It has also afforded the band the ability to have complete creative control over the albums they make and to take some turns over the years, from heavier material (*Train of Thought*) to more progressive and conceptual (*Metropolis Part 2: Scenes from a Memory*).

I have followed the band's career closely ever since Mike Portnoy was a guest on my radio show during the late '90s. One of my favorite DT stories was when the band played Radio City Music Hall for the last show of their twentieth anniversary tour in 2006, documented on the album and DVD *Score*. Portnoy asked me to intro the band—a great honor, especially on the legendary Radio City stage. Because of super-strict union laws, I had to do the intro from behind the curtain. If the theater pulled open the

LEFT: James LaBrie
ABOVE: John Petrucci

EDDIE'S PLAYLIST DREAM THEATER

1. THE ROOT OF ALL EVIL 2. I WALK BESIDE YOU 3. 6:00
4. ENDLESS SACRIFICE 5. CONSTANT MOTION 6. WITHER
7. PULL ME UNDER 8. PANIC ATTACK 9. FORSAKEN 10. AS I AM

TOP: John Myung and Mike Portnoy
BOTTOM: John Petrucci
OPPOSITE: Mike Portnoy

curtain, the venue began to run the clock, thus cutting into the band's set time, so I had to stay behind. Also, I was told that someone on the house staff needed to make announcements before I could introduce the band. So there I was, behind the curtain on one of the most famous stages in the world, while a ninety-year-old guy wearing a jacket and tie announced to the rabid DT fans the upcoming shows at Radio City: Dora the Explorer and the Wiggles. This man clearly had no idea who was playing that night, and needless to say, the place was booing. He then handed me the mic, and when they heard it was my voice the place went nuts! (DT fans know I'm one of the few who play the band's music, so that passion extends beyond the band, thankfully.) Of course, all I had to say was "Ready for some Dream Theater?" The old guy gave me the worst look and just walked off.

Since the band's inception, they have been guided by Petrucci and Portnoy. Even though Myung is also a founding member, he is extremely reserved and quiet. Mike Portnoy and John Petrucci produced many of the band's albums and wrote a large portion of the material. But Portnoy was always the mouthpiece of the band and the one doing the press. Mike likes this role and is good at it. A music fan of many genres, he's also, without question, the band's strongest personality. We've become great friends. Our families have hung out, and he has done my radio and TV shows many times. He's best known for playing a mammoth drum set, and he literally needs to walk around this "drum village" of sorts. But his playing is so special that he can sit behind a tiny kit and be just as impressive. Regardless of whether he's playing some intricate jazz fusion, Who- or Zeppelin-style hard rock, or raging thrash metal, he can truly handle it all equally well.

Mike is also a tireless worker and simply loves to play and create—he wants to do everything with everybody, yesterday! He once even bailed me out and played a set with thrash metal legends Overkill during an event I was throwing when Overkill's drummer couldn't make his flight. In 2011 he paired with guitarist John Sykes and bassist Billy Sheehan for what could have been an amazing power trio. (I have the demos!) But unfortunately, this group was doomed from the start, since Mike and John have totally different work styles. Simply put, Mike Portnoy, given the number of people and bands he's played with, could have his own chapter in this book!

A major swing that reverberated with Dream Theater took place in the spring of 2010 when Portnoy joined Avenged Sevenfold to fill in for deceased drummer Jimmy "the Rev" Sullivan. Sullivan was one of many young players who cited Portnoy as an influence, and the band felt it would be fitting to have Mike fill his drum stool for the album and tour. Mike loved the Avenged gig and felt that after twenty years with Dream Theater, it would be a good time for all the guys to take a break from one another. The tensions that come from being with a group of guys on the road for a couple of decades were starting to show, and Portnoy felt some time apart would help. The problem was, the other members of the band didn't agree, and they wanted Mike to begin working immediately with Dream Theater once again. A standoff ensued, and in September 2010 what many thought could never happen did: Mike Portnoy was out of Dream Theater, a band he not only helped create but also was very much the face of. After a public audition process, Dream Theater replaced Portnoy with current drummer Mike Mangini and released their first album without Portnoy, *A Dramatic Turn of Events,* to generally positive reviews. They also embarked on a lengthy world tour with Mangini behind the kit. As a close friend of Mike's, I did my best to support him through what was a difficult time. A few months later, his gig with Avenged was finished, and that's when it truly hit him that he had lost his band of the past twenty-plus years. But as time has moved forward, I can honestly say that Mike has made peace with his decision. He now can play with so many different bands and musicians and in many styles. He just may be too ambitious and in demand for only one group. Since his departure from Dream Theater, he has been in several bands—from Adrenaline Mob, with its high-energy metal, to a new trio with Billy Sheehan and guitarist/singer Richie Kotzen called the Winery Dogs that I actually helped put together.

Mike Portnoy is a frequent guest on my radio and TV shows, and along with our mutual buddy, WWE star and musician Chris Jericho, we often spend hours talking music in what we call "Metal Summits." Dream Theater continues to thrive with Mangini on board, and the fan base has seemed to embrace the change while still keeping an eye on what Portnoy is up to and supporting his more progressive projects like Flying Colors and Transatlantic. Both Portnoy and Dream Theater have proven that sticking to your guns and doing what you believe in (and being great at it) can really pay off and yield a large and loyal following—no small feat in today's incredibly competitive and fickle music business.

? DID YOU KNOW

Current drummer Mike Mangini was at one time a member of Extreme and Annihilator. He also played on three solo albums with Dream Theater singer James LaBrie: *Keep It to Yourself, James LaBrie's MullMuzzler 2,* and *Elements of Persuasion.*

EXODUS

Many Exodus fans get upset that the band isn't included with the esteemed Big Four of thrash metal (Anthrax, Megadeth, Metallica, and Slayer), and surely they have a case. Exodus was very much an early part of the thrash scene and one of the pioneering acts of the genre. The story of Exodus is certainly one of perseverance in the face of numerous lineup changes, record label issues, shifts in the musical climate, and even the death of one of their singers. And after nearly thirty-five years, Exodus remains one of the most overlooked bands in the development of thrash.

CLASSIC LINEUP:

PAUL BALOFF (VOCALS)

GARY HOLT (GUITAR)

RICK HUNOLT (GUITAR)

TOM HUNTING (DRUMS)

ROB MCKILLOP (BASS)

STEVE SOUZA (VOCALS)

KEY ADDITIONAL MEMBERS:

LEE ALTUS (GUITAR)

ROB DUKES (VOCALS)

JACK GIBSON (BASS)

KIRK HAMMETT (GUITAR)

JOHN TEMPESTA (DRUMS)

OPPOSITE: Rob Dukes, Gary Holt, and Jack Gibson

DISCOGRAPHY

BONDED BY BLOOD (1985)

PLEASURES OF THE FLESH
(1987)

FABULOUS DISASTER (1989)

IMPACT IS IMMINENT (1990)

FORCE OF HABIT (1992)

TEMPO OF THE DAMNED
(2004)

*SHOVEL HEADED
KILL MACHINE* (2005)

*THE ATROCITY EXHIBITION:
EXHIBIT A* (2007)

LET THERE BE BLOOD (2008)

*EXHIBIT B:
THE HUMAN CONDITION*
(2010)

ABOVE: Rick Hunolt and Rob Dukes
RIGHT: Rick Hunolt, Tom Hunting, Gary
Holt, Paul Baloff, and Rob McKillop
OPPOSITE: Gary Holt

The band began in the very active San Francisco Bay Area thrash scene of the early '80s. Along with guitarist Gary Holt and drummer Tom Hunting, a then-unknown guitarist named Kirk Hammett got his start playing in Exodus, and even named the band after a novel he had read. The earliest years saw the usual upheaval and growth that any young group experiences. But even then, Exodus had a reputation as an incredible live act. They were influenced by British bands like Motörhead and Judas Priest, and similarly their music added in the energy and speed of punk, causing such an aggressive frenzy in the crowd that it had to be seen to be believed. Stage diving, broken bones, and bloody noses were the norm at Exodus performances.

The band had its first of many major shifts when in early 1983 Hammett announced his departure from Exodus to join Metallica. Hammett replaced Dave Mustaine on the eve of Metallica's recording its debut album, *Kill 'Em All*. Kirk later told me that it was an incredibly tough decision for him at the time. Exodus was very much his baby, and he had put a great deal of work into the band during those early years, including playing on the band's first demo in 1981, his only recorded history with the band. Leaving something he was instrumental in building from day one, for a band in which he would be viewed as a replacement member, was a risky choice. But the allure of the buzz on Metallica and the chance to jump right into the studio to record was too hard to resist—and clearly history has shown us how wise Kirk was.

Exodus replaced Hammett with Rick Hunolt and recorded their debut with vocalist Paul Baloff. *Bonded by Blood* was made in 1984 but not properly released until April 1985 because of business and label issues. The album was very well received, and its raw edge gave a great representation of what Exodus did live. The timeline here is important to note, because even though Exodus was formed in 1980, around the same time as their Big Four contemporaries, it took five years for their debut to hit store shelves. By this time, Metallica, Megadeth, Slayer, and Anthrax already

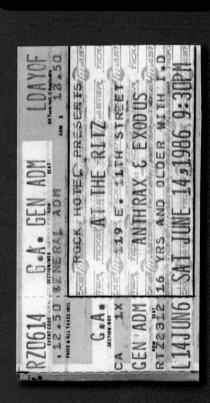
had a couple of albums and national tours under their belts. Exodus's slow start is one of the reasons why they're not included with the Big Four of this genre, even though they were right there at its inception.

Finally up and running with a debut album and tour, Exodus began to record *Bonded by Blood*'s follow-up. But while making the demos for the album that would eventually become 1987's *Pleasures of the Flesh*, the other band members clashed with Baloff, resulting in the firing of their singer after just one album and tour. Needless to say, this was not the way the band wanted to start their career—losing two key members in a relatively short period of time. Baloff was replaced by Steve "Zetro" Souza, who left another upstart Bay Area thrash band called Legacy

ABOVE: Rick Hunolt

(later renamed Testament) and handled vocals for the band's sophomore release. *Fabulous Disaster* followed in 1989 and gave Exodus the closest shot they ever had to a crossover hit with "The Toxic Waltz." The thrash scene exploded, and they landed a major-label deal with Capitol Records. It really looked like the time had arrived for Exodus—they were a sought-after band to see live and "The Toxic Waltz" was getting regular play on MTV and some radio. But just as they seemed poised to take that leap into the big leagues, the changing musical climate crushed their chances.

What is often forgotten about when people speak of the rise of grunge in the early '90s is that in killing the '80s "hair bands" (I hate that term, but you know what I mean), it also knocked the hell out of *all* the hard rock and metal of the day. Even bands that weren't MTV darlings and didn't rock the spandex and makeup took a big hit, especially the bands still working hard to break big—like Exodus. For 1992's *Force of Habit*, Exodus changed their style, moving away from faster-tempo material and more toward slower Sabbath-type songs. Response to the album was mixed. This, coupled with the emergence of the Seattle sound, hurt the group, and a hiatus was announced. For about ten years, Exodus remained nearly dormant, with the exception of some live recordings. It wasn't until 2001 that Exodus reunited live for a Bay Area benefit for Testament singer Chuck Billy called Thrash of the Titans. But just when it appeared that Exodus would be reborn, tragedy struck. Singer Paul Baloff suffered a stroke in early 2002, which led to his untimely death. Steve Souza returned to Exodus for a brief time as the band tried to re-establish itself, and finally they reached some level of stability with the arrival of vocalist Rob Dukes in 2005. Dukes continues to front the band to this day.

Exodus made some solid albums in the 2000s, including *Shovel Headed Kill Machine* and *Exhibit B: The Human Condition*. But in 2011 it was announced that guitarist Gary Holt, the only person to appear on every Exodus album, was joining Slayer temporarily to replace guitarist Jeff Hanneman, who was suffering from a massive infection in his arm due to a spider bite and was unable to play. At the time of writing, Holt has been performing with Slayer for more than two years. Questions about when Hanneman will return and what Holt's future will hold are topics of great speculation in metal circles. In early 2012, all the key members of Exodus (including Hammett) performed at a Paul Baloff memorial concert in Oakland, California, marking the first time they had shared a stage together in thirty years.

Despite all the change-ups, Exodus has a tremendous amount of love from their die-hard fans and respect from the metal community. I like to compare them to another overlooked thrash band with incredible talent: Overkill. Overkill is to the East Coast what Exodus is to the West Coast—very strong in their home markets without enough national crossover. There is no question that Exodus has suffered a wide array of setbacks throughout their history, but they continue to be one of the premier bands in thrash metal, and what lies ahead is anyone's guess.

Drummer John Tempesta landed the gig in Exodus when the band was on tour with Anthrax. Tempesta was originally the drum tech for Anthrax's Charlie Benante, whose kit he was playing during a sound-check when Exodus heard him and thought he'd be the perfect replacement for Tom Hunting.

ABOVE: Rob McKillop and Paul Baloff

EXTREME

It's tragic that some people don't realize what an incredibly ass-kicking band Extreme is. This is, of course, due to the fact that neither of the band's two massive hit singles ("More Than Words" and "Hole Hearted") was truly indicative of their real sound. I've talked to the band members about this many times, and while it's hard to say that having massive crossover hits is a negative, Extreme has been fighting the perception that they're a group of crooners ever since. I would describe their music as a cross between the big melodies of Queen and the hard rock of Van Halen—with a funky rhythm section underneath. But mention Extreme to someone in the hard rock community who has never seen the band live or listened to one of their full albums, and you will get a roll of the eyes, as if Extreme doesn't belong in the conversation of truly great hard rock bands. Let me tell you, they do.

CLASSIC LINEUP:

PAT BADGER (BASS)

NUNO BETTENCOURT (GUITAR)

GARY CHERONE (VOCALS)

PAUL GEARY (DRUMS)

KEY ADDITIONAL MEMBERS:

KEVIN FIGUEIREDO (DRUMS)

MIKE MANGINI (DRUMS)

DISCOGRAPHY

Extreme first came together in the Boston area in the mid-'80s with the original lineup of Gary Cherone on vocals, Nuno Bettencourt on guitar, Pat Badger on bass, and Paul Geary on drums. The band specialized in super-high-energy live shows, dynamic harmonies, incredible guitar playing, and hard rock that was heavy on groove. Seeing these early Extreme shows gave a sense of how hungry this band was for success. They worked the stage nonstop, and had a megastar guitarist in Nuno Bettencourt. Nuno could play it all with flash and fire, and had an ability that quickly branded him a rising guitar hero at the time. The dynamics of the vocals were another secret weapon. Nuno, Pat, and, of course, Gary all sang incredibly well, giving the band the added pop of huge choruses and hooks that they could truly deliver live. It wasn't long before the labels started venturing to New England to see what all the fuss was about. Extreme had built a great following by gigging in the region and winning "Best Band" at the Boston Music Awards two years in a row ('86 and '87). They signed to A&M Records in 1988 and released their self-titled debut one year later.

Extreme captured some of the same energy of the band's live shows and served as a good introduction to the group's funky hard rock and Nuno's fretboard fireworks. The band scored some radio and video play with the lead single "Kid Ego" and the follow-up "Mutha (Don't Wanna Go to School Today)," but the real track that had people talking was the album's closer, "Play with Me." With its breakneck pace and riffing, "Play with Me" was the ultimate showcase for Nuno and was included in the film *Bill and Ted's Excellent Adventure*. But the debut album also signaled to fans that although Extreme certainly had some of the elements of the look and sound of the time, the band also had diverse qualities that were more in line with Queen and Led Zeppelin, and a sound that could be hard to categorize. Extreme wasn't afraid to use horns and acoustic breakdowns, and even to write conceptual pieces. To put it simply, Extreme had more

DID YOU KNOW

Extreme performed at the Freddie Mercury tribute concert in London in 1992. They are huge Queen fans, and it is one of their all-time highlights as a band. Brian May introduced them as a new group that truly understood what Queen was about.

going on than most other bands of the day, could play circles around many of them, and were never afraid to try different sounds and styles.

The debut did a good job at getting the word out and gained enough of an audience to warrant a follow-up, *Extreme II: Pornograffitti*, released in 1990. Right from the opening track, "Decadence Dance," it was obvious they were making a big leap forward. The song starts with the sounds of a thunderstorm, then some piano, and moves to some stomping before building into a monster Nuno riff. The overall guitar sounds on the album were much bigger than those on the debut. I was a huge fan of *Pornograffitti* from the start, and I loved how everything jumped right out at you. Subtitled "A Funked Up Fairy Tale," it raised the game for Extreme, making everything epic. Producer Michael Wagener, who had worked with Ozzy, Metallica, and many others, helped give a new charge to a band that was already super-high energy.

The lead singles "Decadence Dance" and "Get the Funk Out" failed to have any major chart impact, and the album wasn't performing. But with the release of the album's third single, "More Than Words," everything changed for Extreme. This folky, acoustic ballad with striking harmonies—which really featured only Gary and Nuno—became a surprise smash hit and seemingly overnight had a whole new audience talking about Extreme. Suddenly a big loud hard rock band was all over MTV and being played on easy-listening and rock radio. I clearly remember working in a record store and having older people come in for an album called *Pornograffitti* because it had this beautiful love song they were hearing on the radio. (And several tried to return the album when they realized pretty much everything else on it was hard blazing guitar rock!) "More Than Words" reached number one on the pop charts and was followed up with the album's only other acoustic track, "Hole Hearted," which went to number four. Extreme was huge, but it was from the success of two acoustic ballads that had little to do with what the band was about.

LEFT: Pat Badger, Kevin Figueiredo, and Nuno Bettencourt
ABOVE: Paul Geary
OPPOSITE LEFT: Pat Badger
OPPOSITE RIGHT: Gary Cherone

1. TELL ME SOMETHING I DON'T KNOW 2. PORNOGRAFFITTI
3. WHEN I'M PRESIDENT 4. DECADENCE DANCE 5. WARHEADS
6. THERE IS NO GOD 7. LEARN TO LOVE 8. PLAY WITH ME
9. CUPID'S DEAD 10. WIND ME UP

EDDIE'S PLAYLIST EXTREME

TOP: Gary Cherone and Eddie
BOTTOM: Nuno Bettencourt
OPPOSITE: Gary Cherone
and Nuno Bettencourt

III Sides to Every Story, released in 1992, was a concept album of sorts, featuring elaborate production and conceptual videos. But it just didn't connect and failed to score any major hits—a surprise after the monster success of *Pornograffitti*. Some hard rock fans had lost interest in Extreme after the band connected to the housewife crowd with "More Than Words," and *III Sides* featured some longer tracks that were mostly shunned by rock radio. Even though it's a very solid and at times complex hard rock album, it couldn't please either side of the group's audience. Factor in the changing climate for '80s-based rock music as the mid-'90s rolled around, and you had a band that was viewed as old news just a year after having two Top 5 hits.

In 1994, drummer Paul Geary announced his decision to leave Extreme and pursue a career as an artist manager, at which he became very successful. Geary was replaced by phenomenal player Mike Mangini (now in Dream Theater), and Extreme recorded their fourth album, *Waiting for the Punchline*. This was a darker and angrier-sounding record. The lead single, a track called "Hip Today," was a statement about where they stood as a band in 1995 versus the other "cooler" grunge bands of the time—with a chorus that warned "You'll be gone tomorrow." The record sounded a bit dry at times but still featured great songs and playing. I really liked where the band was heading musically and had them on my radio show to discuss the new album. When I saw Gary and Nuno that day, I could tell they knew they were in for an uphill climb. Their music was out of fashion, and radio, which had loved them, now had no time for Extreme. They visited me at the studio that afternoon for a prerecorded interview, but were never invited on with the live DJ that day. Extreme was old news to many, and a year later they were pretty much gone.

With the ending of Extreme, singer Gary Cherone joined Van Halen for a brief time and also released his own albums while fronting the bands Tribe of Judah and Hurtsmile. Bassist Pat Badger dropped out of music

for a bit and raised alpacas. Nuno released a solo album and a couple of albums with the bands Mourning Widows (which I highly recommend), DramaGods, and Satellite Party (with Jane's Addiction's Perry Farrell), as well as several others. For years, Gary tried to lure his partner back to Extreme, and Nuno finally agreed in 2008. A new Extreme studio album, *Saudades de Rock*, was released, and the band hit the road again with new drummer Kevin Figueiredo on tours with King's X and Ratt. I hosted a show with Extreme in 2009, and they were as incredible as I remembered them in their prime. This was documented on the 2010 live release *Take Us Alive*.

Just as Extreme was starting to reestablish its rock fan base, Nuno accepted a gig as a guitarist in pop star Rihanna's band. Touring the world in arenas again was too good of an offer (and paycheck) to turn down. Gary was clearly not happy at the time, as he had just started up again with his longtime partner, then lost him, but he understood the decision and did his best to keep himself busy musically while waiting for Bettencourt to return. In 2011, I had Gary on my radio show to talk about Nuno being off in pop-land, and we decided to call him and break his balls. Nuno answered the phone even though he was sound asleep in Germany. He was a good sport about the call and assured everyone that Extreme would

LITA FORD

Although Lita Ford is commonly viewed as an '80s artist, her career dates back to the mid-'70s, when, at just sixteen years old, she was recruited to be a part of an all-female rock group that producer Kim Fowley was putting together called the Runaways. The band had a relatively short life-span, lasting just four years, but two of its members had major success as solo performers after the breakup: Joan Jett and Lita Ford. While Joan took her solo career in a more punk direction, Lita went metal. Look no further than the cover of her 1983 solo debut, *Out for Blood*, on which she's clad in leather, smoke rising from her feet, her hair sprayed out, with a black guitar in her hands. It sent a clear message that Lita was leaving the pop-flavored hard rock of the Runaways behind for a much harder assault.

CLASSIC LINEUP:

**LITA FORD
(GUITAR/VOCALS)**

DISCOGRAPHY

Although *Out for Blood* was far from a major success, it established Lita as one of the few female singers and guitarists in the metal genre. Some close-minded listeners were skeptical of Lita's ability to play. Was it really her? Could a woman really play guitar as well as the guys who dominated the rock landscape at the time? The answer was YES. Lita was never just a pretty face with her trademark B.C. Rich as a prop. She was dedicated to her playing, which showcased a melodic style but had some flash and fireworks to keep it interesting.

On her follow-up release, *Dancin' on the Edge*, she kept her metal sound, but her hooks and playing got stronger, and the album's opener "Gotta Let Go," even gained some radio and MTV play. Lita finally got the hits she'd been chasing since her teenage days with her 1988 album simply called *Lita*, on her new label RCA Records. Again, she still had her metal image, but the music was more polished and commercial, thanks to the arrival of producer Mike Chapman (whose résumé included albums by Blondie and the Knack) and manager Sharon Osbourne. Outside song writers contributed to craft some hits, and stylists were employed to give Lita the look of the moment.

Lita's more accessible sound and her looks were a perfect fit for MTV and suddenly she was all over the TV and radio. And Lita knew how to work it! She played the metal sex kitten role to the max in her videos—licking ice cubes, rolling around on the floor, and most important, still rocking. It was a unique and powerful combination for the time. Lita became an in-demand music star not only by fans but also by the industry, which regarded her as the First Lady of Heavy Metal. She was also known for being in some high-profile relationships: with Tony Iommi of Black Sabbath, Chris Holmes of W.A.S.P., and Nikki Sixx of Mötley Crüe. Everyone wanted to get close to Lita. And the success of the *Lita* album made 1988 a banner year, scoring her hit singles and videos for "Kiss Me Deadly," "Back to the Cave," and the duet with Ozzy Osbourne, "Close My Eyes Forever," which became a Top 10 hit. I was happy to see the success Lita was having at the time. It was refreshing to see a female artist break through in the male-dominated world of heavy metal, but the music was a bit glossy for my tastes. She looked hard rock but the songs on this album, unlike her earlier ones, were more in line with pop. To me, it seemed to hark back to the Runaways days—a bit too manufactured.

I may not have been the only one who felt Lita was getting a bit too polished for the hard rock crowd, as *Lita* became her only true hit album. The 1990 follow-up, *Stiletto*, was even more commercial sounding and failed

DID YOU KNOW ?

The 2010 film *The Runaways* barely featured references to Lita Ford. Lita's and Joan Jett's management, the latter of which was behind the film, clashed on how she would be represented, and therefore much of her story line wasn't included in the motion picture.

Florida. It was there that Lita and Jim raised two sons. Not wanting to be a mother who was on the road and immersed in the rock scene, Lita left music behind for more than ten years to raise her children in a postcard environment and in a home that didn't even have a TV. She decided that it was time to get back into recording and performing only when her sons were old enough to come on the road with her and see what a cool rocker mom she was.

It was around 2008 that I first heard through an agent that Lita was getting back into music. Fans had long been asking me what had happened to her, and so she decided to do one of her first post-"retirement" radio interviews with me to announce her comeback. When it came time

LEFT: Lita Ford

EDDIE'S PLAYLIST
LITA FORD

1. GOTTA LET GO
2. CAN'T CATCH ME
3. FALLING IN AND OUT OF LOVE
4. LIVING LIKE A RUNAWAY
5. OUT FOR BLOOD
6. SHOT OF POISON
7. DRESSED TO KILL
8. CLOSE MY EYES FOREVER
9. BACK TO THE CAVE
10. KISS ME DEADLY

⏮   ▶❙❙   ⏭

ABOVE AND RIGHT: Lita Ford

to shoot a pilot for *That Metal Show* and we needed a guest, I knew Lita would be ideal. Nobody had seen her for ages, and it would make for great TV. She was the first-ever guest on *TMS*, and fans truly loved that she was back. When she started playing live shows again, her family was with her every step of the way, with husband Jim steering the ship and acting as her manager. Jim played up Lita's past sex symbol role and even came out and sang with her. They were almost like a heavy metal Sonny and Cher! Under the heavy direction of her husband, Lita made her first album of new studio material in almost twenty years, 2009's *Wicked Wonderland*. But the album was not what Lita Ford fans were hoping for, and it was poorly received. Gillette had tried to mold his wife into a more modern rocker (think Lita Ford trying to be Rob Zombie). Still, "The Lita and Jim Show" was everywhere, even touring with Queensrÿche (who at times, bizarrely, backed Lita and Jim onstage). What nobody knew at the time, though, was that Lita felt pressured into much of this against her better judgment.

Lita has since claimed that due to her complicated relationship with Gillette, she went along with his concepts for her music and image. I had dinner with her shortly after their breakup, and she was in a very bad place at the time—her children were living with their father and she was also trying to get over the negative reception of her comeback album. But Lita is a trooper, and as I was trying to encourage her that she could get her life (and her fans) back, she put her fork down on the plate, looked me square in the eyes, and said, "You're right, Eddie. I'm coming back, Tina Turner style." I'll never forget it, and I could see the determination in her face. I knew she would try to give her fans a true Lita Ford comeback album.

Lita teamed up with guitarist Gary Hoey and started sending me new tracks as they completed them. Because we had become friends and she knew that I had an idea of what her fans would love to hear, she asked for my input. The tracks were strong, more in line with the classic hard rock she had been making in the early '80s but with an updated feel. There was emotion in the album that came directly from the ugly divorce and custody battle that still hangs over her. The album was released in 2012 and appropriately titled *Living Like a Runaway*, a reference to her first band and the situation she currently found herself in. The title track is an instant Lita classic that tells her life story in about five minutes. Another track, "Mother," is an emotionally charged message to her estranged sons. The entire album is raw and personal and one of her best. She went on tour later that year opening for Def Leppard, and fans welcomed back the new/old Lita with open arms. Even though she still has much to recover from, she is forging ahead, and I'm proud of her resilience.

ABOVE: Lita Ford
LEFT: Eddie and Lita Ford

ACE FREHLEY

My story, and eventual friendship, with Ace Frehley is one that is hard to believe when you consider what a major Kiss fan I was growing up. As documented in my first book, Kiss was the band that started it all for me back in 1976 while I was still in junior high school. So it's surreal for me to look back on how one of the band's founding members has become one of my closest friends for the past twenty-five years.

CLASSIC LINEUP:

**ACE FREHLEY
(GUITAR/VOCALS)**

OPPOSITE: Ace Frehley

DISCOGRAPHY

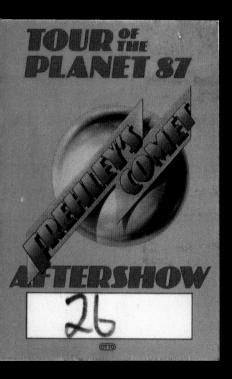

knew him. What I loved most about his playing was his guitar tone and how his solos were often songs within the songs. There was a melodi sense to his playing that you could just sing—an amazing quality ver few musicians have had before or since. Is he the most technically gifte player of all time? No. But his solos mean something in almost every song he plays. There's also the flashy and innovative guitar effects that he cre ated while in Kiss and that he still uses: the smoking guitar, the rocke shooting guitar, the flashing guitar. These were all amazing things in thei day and an extension of the Spaceman persona he created. It honestl boggles my mind that Kiss has another player dress as Ace and imperson ate him today (and some fans just look the other way). That's not comin from "Eddie, the friend of Ace"; that's coming from "Eddie, the lifelon Kiss fan"! Ace is unique in every way, and no matter who impersonate him, there is only one true Ace Frehley.

In 1986 I landed a gig working for the legendary metal label Megaforc Records, known for bringing Anthrax, Metallica, Overkill, and many mor to the music world. Once I came on board, my goal was to bring in an ac that could get some radio play and cross over to both hard rock and meta fans. Johnny Z, who owned the label, was never a Kiss fan, but one da when having a conversation with him, I told him we should track down Ac Frehley. I explained to Johnny that Ace was a guy who many fans won dered about but few had ever seen after he left Kiss in 1983. But Ace wa considered a high risk. The loose canon in Kiss with drugs and booze, wh was once even chased by cops while driving the wrong way on the road Ace was a liability few labels wanted to take a chance on, despite knowin fans would love a new solo album from him. His 1978 solo album with Kis yielded the only hit from the four members' simultaneous solo release "New York Groove." I knew Ace could bring Megaforce to a new level, an Johnny Z was game, but how was I supposed to contact the guy?

After leaving Kiss, Ace had done gigs with his band Frehley's Come with various lineups. The shows were always packed, and I had seen a fe myself. There was always a reckless danger in the room—with high-energ hard rock played fast, loose, and loud. But there never seemed to be an game plan to release an album or tour on a national level. I eventuall tracked down Ace through producer Eddie Kramer, who was working wit Megaforce act Anthrax and had produced Ace both with Kiss and sol Kramer said Ace had some solid demos and set up a lunch meeting for u in New York City. My exterior played it cool (just having a tuna sandwic with a possible client), but on the inside I was geeking out! We had alread heard the demos and knew the material was there, and Ace assured u there were more great songs to come. He also told us he was sober, whic had been a huge concern for everyone. The meeting went well, and ne thing you know, I'm in the label's lawyer's office signing the former lea guitarist of the band that changed my life.

Up to this point, Ace's solo group had been billed as Frehley's Come but everyone felt Ace's name should be front and center. So the grou

I was on the road once with Ace in 1988 in Austin, Texas, and we were walking around town after his gig and saw that a Kiss tribute band was playing a local club. I suggested that we walk in and that Ace should shock the band and crowd by going onstage. He did! I will never forget the look on the face of the tribute band's "Ace" as the real Ace asked if he could use his Les Paul and play a couple of tunes.

There is a photo inside the jacket of Ace's *Second Sighting* album of two feet turned different ways. Those feet are mine!

In 2011, Ace released his autobiography, called *No Regrets*. In it, he tells the story of me resuscitating him with a fish sandwich. You'll have to read it to learn more of that story!

LEFT: Ace Frehley

ACE FREHLEY

Just 4 Fun Tour
Summer '93

6/25

(ALL ACCESS)   LOCAL CREW

AFTER SHOW ONLY   PHOTO ONLY

EDDIE'S PLAYLIST

ACE FREHLEY

1. GIVE IT TO ME ANYWAY
2. TROUBLE WALKIN'
3. ROCK SOLDIERS
4. RIP IT OUT
5. OZONE

6. SHOT FULL OF ROCK
7. 2 YOUNG 2 DIE
8. SNOW BLIND
9. BREAKOUT
10. SISTER

ABOVE: Ace Frehley

was simply called "Ace Frehley" on the first album, *Frehley's Comet*. The group itself went through a fairly major change. For the past three or four years, Ace's right hand had been singer/guitarist Richie Scarlet, a powerhouse performer, singer, and player with a Keith Richards look. He was the perfect counterpart to Ace, so we were all shocked when Ace announced he wanted to replace Richie prior to recording. It just seemed like Ace wanted some new blood. Ace asked me for suggestions for a new singer/guitarist—the first of many times he would ask for my counsel over the years. At first, I suggested Derek St. Holmes, who had filled a similar role for Ted Nugent. Derek came down for a jam, but it didn't click. Then I remembered a band called 707 from the San Francisco Bay Area who had a singer/guitarist/keyboardist by the name of Tod Howarth. I didn't know Tod at the time, but thought he could do it all. I sent Ace the 707 album titled, coincidentally, *Mega Force*. Next thing I knew, Tod was a member of the first recording lineup of Ace Frehley. Tod had done some work with Cheap Trick and Ted Nugent and was also on bassist John Regan's radar. The lineup was rounded out by bassist Regan (who had played with Peter Frampton and was an early member of Frehley's Comet) and drummer Anton Fig. Anton is known these days as David Letterman's drummer but had worked with Kiss uncredited and also played on Ace's '78 solo album. The debut album *Frehley's Comet*, which Eddie Kramer produced, came out in 1987 and was a collection of songs both old and new. "Rock Soldiers," an autobiographical tale of Ace's life and mishaps, has the memorable line "Ace is back and he told you so," which serves as the theme for the entire album. Howarth sings lead vocals on two of the album's songs: a song written for Kiss but never used called "Breakout" and another named "Calling to You," which was actually a rewrite of the song "Mega Force" from Tod's 707 album. Everyone felt it would be a bit cheesy to have a song with the same title as the record company's name, so it was revised for Ace's album. *Frehley's Comet* sold very well. Videos were shot for the lead single, "Into the Night," and the follow-up, "Rock Soldiers," and they received some MTV play. The album came very close to going gold and quickly became one of the label's biggest sellers. Ace was indeed back, and he kept his promise of sobriety, at least for the moment. I was so proud, both as a young label A&R guy and as a Kiss fan.

But things unraveled fast for Ace. He was on the road and back to the rock-and-roll lifestyle. John Regan played a huge role in keeping things on track. He was more than a bass player; he was someone who kept an eye on Ace and tried to be a good influence. Regan always had the band's and Ace's best interests at heart, but it was getting hard to keep Ace on the straight and narrow. I'm ignorant of drug use, because I don't have experience with it, but something was clearly up. Our parent label, Atlantic, wanted another studio album from Ace, and a tour was booked for the band to open for Iron Maiden. I knew Ace wasn't ready with new material, but the label demanded an album. Since Ace wasn't in a position to write, Tod saw this as his opportunity to come in with a ton of songs. Tod's material was good and he has a great voice, but the fans wanted to hear Ace. Still, there was little choice. I was enlisted as an executive producer, and we took the best of what Ace had and filled in the balance with Tod's songs and vocals. The album was recorded by Regan, Howarth, and drummer Jamie Oldaker, who was from Eric Clapton's band. I went to the studio many times to check in on the progress, and Ace was rarely there. One day, Ace showed up and he was a mess. I'll never forget him sitting down to cut a solo while eating a bagel with cream cheese and having it explode when he bit into it, with the guitar in his lap and cream cheese oozing through the strings. Needless to say, I was worried about him.

Ace was certainly on the album, called *Second Sighting*, but this time the band was billed as Frehley's Comet, not Ace Frehley. There was no time for album cover art, so we just licensed a photo of a planet from NASA and slapped it on. I chose a song called "Insane" as the lead single, since it was the best track with Ace on lead vocals. But the album was the least "Ace," missing his usual heavy sound, and it suffered for it. So for the third studio album, everyone agreed it was time to get Richie Scarlet back. Tod was a huge asset, but he wanted to be a bit more involved in the band's image and sound when we had to go back to selling Ace. Album three wasn't billed as Frehley's Comet but rather as Ace Frehley again. *Trouble Walkin'*, released in 1989, was a great comeback. Scarlet brought the energy and attitude on his tracks, and Ace's material was

UNDERGROUND CLASSIC

The 1997 compilation *Loaded Deck* features a previously unreleased track originally written in the early '80s called "Give It to Me Anyway." It was recorded for *Trouble Walkin'* but left off the album. It features lead vocals by Richie Scarlet as well as guest appearances by Peter Criss and Skid Row. It's one of my favorite tracks. Ace also appears on Anton Fig's 2002 solo album, *Figments*, on a track called "Know Where You Go."

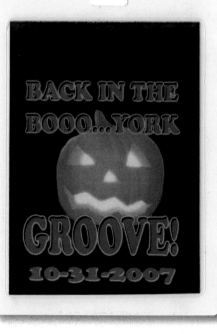

strong again. Even Eddie Kramer returned to the producing chair, and we called in Peter Criss one day to sing and play some percussion. At the time, I had introduced Ace to a new band just signed to Atlantic called Skid Row. Huge Ace fans, they came down to sing some backup vocals. Ace made a killer record, but it was the album that should have come after the debut. Therefore sales weren't strong, and the idea to release the band doing a cover of ELO's "Do Ya" wasn't smart. Shortly after the album was released, I left the label and so did Ace. It would be twenty years until he released a new studio album.

In 2006, I was working as a producer for a VH1 show called *Rock Honors*, which was honoring Kiss. Tommy Thayer, dressed as Ace and playing his parts, was being honored with the band. I suggested that since the show was honoring *Kiss*, Ace should jam with them. But Gene and Paul refused. So instead, I helped assemble a tribute band that would also play, including Rob Zombie, Tommy Lee, Scott Ian, Gilby Clarke, and Slash. Since Ace wasn't allowed to play with Kiss, he joined the all-star tribute band. It wasn't easy watching Ace playing without makeup in a tribute to the band he helped create, while a guy impersonating him played with Kiss! But we made the most of the night, and in the end, Ace was glad to be a part of it and leave others to question why Kiss wouldn't let him play with them.

Ace later began work on a new solo album with various people at his home studio in Connecticut. He called me one day to have a listen and see if I could provide some direction. I sat in his studio listening to endless riffs and song ideas featuring many different musicians, and the biggest issue I saw was that Ace needed a producer, someone to crack the whip and shape the material. So Ace enlisted producers and engineers Marti Frederiksen and Anthony Focx to come on board and mix the album. Eventually, in 2009, *Anomaly* was released. It ended up being mostly a collection of older unreleased songs that were recorded, as well as some newly written material and a cover of Sweet's "Fox on the Run." Since it was his first solo album in twenty years, he dedicated it to late Kiss drummer Eric Carr and late Pantera guitarist Dimebag Darrell, who had a tattoo of Ace on his chest. I really liked the album, and so did most Ace fans, which got Ace's juices flowing—and got him working on a follow-up.

Usually, when people stop working together in the music world, they drift apart. But Ace and I had a strong bond. We stayed in touch, and in some ways became even closer friends. (Those stories and memories are for another book!) But what is most meaningful is knowing the man who Ace has become over the past five years. The light finally went on for Ace, and he got sober and became a changed man and a new and improved human being. He was a blast to drink and party with back in the day, but if that hadn't changed, I know he wouldn't be here. As I have told him many times, even with all his musical achievements, I am most proud of his sobriety and the person he is today. (And he's still a hell of a guitar player, too!)

ABOVE AND OPPOSITE: Ace Frehley

GREAT WHITE

Great White is often erroneously called a metal band, when, in reality, they have very little to do with that genre of music. Early on, they dabbled in edgier fare, and once even toured as an opening act for Judas Priest. But for me, the band's sound has always screamed the blues.

CLASSIC LINEUP:

AUDIE DESBROW (DRUMS)

MARK KENDALL (GUITAR)

MICHAEL LARDIE (KEYBOARDS/GUITAR)

TONY MONTANA (BASS)

JACK RUSSELL (VOCALS)

KEY ADDITIONAL MEMBERS:

LORNE BLACK (BASS)

TEDDY COOK (BASS)

TERRY ILOUS (VOCALS)

SEAN MCNABB (BASS)

SCOTT SNYDER (BASS)

OPPOSITE: Jack Russell and Mark Kendall

DISCOGRAPHY

Vocalist Jack Russell formed Great White in 1977 with guitarist Mark Kendall. The band was originally called Dante Fox, but after a few years changed its name to Great White, which is how Russell used to introduce Kendall onstage, because Kendall often wore white clothes that matched his white hair and white Fender Telecaster (and because Russell was a shark aficionado). The band knocked around the L.A. club scene before things started to heat up. They recorded an EP, and their manager was able to convince local rock radio stations in Southern California to play it. Naturally, this provided a huge lift to their live draw, and in 1983 they scored a major-label deal with EMI.

This was right around the time that I started in radio. As a young metalhead, I loved what I heard when I was sent a single for the hard rocker "Stick It," off their full-length, self-titled 1984 release. It had a catchy riff, a huge shouting chorus, and a great singer in Russell, who memorably spit out the lyrics "crankin' the metal" in his gravelly voice in the song's verse. That song and album remain, by far, the most metal thing the band has created to date, and looking back on it now, I can see that they were probably a reaction to the explosion of successful metal bands of the day. Otherwise, Great White's music had a more classic feel to it, and the influence of British bands like Led Zeppelin, Humble Pie, and Bad Company was apparent. So while Great White had some of the signatures of a metal band on the rise, it wasn't long before they showed their more melodic, bluesy, and Zeppelin-tinged hard rock colors—a great foundation for Russell's phenomenal vocals.

Their true sound became even more apparent with the 1987 release of Once Bitten . . . and its massive hit song "Rock Me." The nearly seven-minute-long track was edited for radio and MTV, but sent a message loud

and clear: Great White was a different beast from other bands of the time. Great White's almost jazzlike approach was on full display on this track, with Russell's soulful vocals, mellow verses, and instrumentals (including a harmonica!) kicking into a big hard-rocking chorus featuring an extended guitar solo from Kendall. Its more organic, blues-based hard rock sound distinguished it from the pop metal anthems all over radio and MTV. Even though Great White started to adopt some of the fashions of the day and often toured with chart-dominating bands like Bon Jovi and others, to me, Great White was on a bit of a different trip. Their bluesy roots gave them broader appeal, crossing over to the hard rock and classic rock crowd, and even to some of the metal holdovers (like me) from the band's beginnings. Soon, they scored a second big hit with the ballad "Save Your Love." Though they had been kicking around for ten years, Great White finally hit the big time with massive sales, nationwide radio play, and constant rotation on MTV. Things got even bigger in 1989 with the release of . . . *Twice Shy* and a cover of Mott the Hoople's "Once Bitten Twice Shy." A few years earlier, Quiet Riot had dipped into a British rock band's catalog (Slade's) and scored a hit ("Cum on Feel the Noize"), and Great White did the same, also making their version of the song far bigger in the United States than the original. Millions of albums sold, with major tours and Grammy nominations following, and before you knew it, Great White was everywhere. But as with most bands that made their mark in the '80s on radio and MTV, Great White saw its fortunes change in the next decade.

By the beginning of the '90s, the members had been touring hard for almost a decade, and partying even harder. Their activities weren't nearly as well publicized in the press as Mötley Crüe's or Guns N' Roses', but by

EDDIE'S PLAYLIST
GREAT WHITE

1. HOUSE OF BROKEN LOVE
2. SAVE YOUR LOVE
3. LADY RED LIGHT
4. FACE THE DAY
5. MISTA BONE
6. SITUATION
7. ROLLIN' STONED
8. ROCK ME
9. STICK IT
10. ON YOUR KNEES

|◀◀   ▶|| ▶▶|

LEFT: Michael Lardie
ABOVE: Mark Kendall
OPPOSITE LEFT: Teddy Cook
OPPOSITE RIGHT: Audie Desbrow

all accounts, Great White was right there with them in terms of rock-and-roll excess. The follow-up albums *Hooked* and *Psycho City* saw declining sales, and soon Mark Kendall became the first victim of the band's hard-partying lifestyle—he was hospitalized for alcoholism and then entered rehab. Kendall was soon replaced by Al Pitrelli, setting off a revolving door of members. The next ten years saw many come and go from the band, which struggled to find an audience in a rock landscape where they were wrongly labeled as just another '80s hair band. By 2000, Jack Russell was the lone original member of Great White, and in 2001 he announced that he was done. He and a recovered Kendall performed a final farewell show before going their own ways.

The years had been hard on Jack, who was struggling with his own addictions, but even still, he took his own version of the band on the road in search of an audience, playing small clubs to often much smaller crowds. Even though he was performing under the name Jack Russell's Great White, most promoters continued to bill them as Great White, hoping to draw in crowds based on the original band's former success. This version of Great White rolled into West Warwick, Rhode Island, and played a nightclub called the Station on the tragic date of February 20, 2003.

As the band took the stage that night, a small blast of Roman candle fireworks was discharged as part of the show's effects. The venue, however, seemed unequipped for such a display. The back wall of the stage caught fire, which spread rapidly, sending the few hundred assembled fans running for the exits. The ensuing panic trapped many in the club, and in the end, one hundred people, including the band's guitarist Ty Longley, lost their lives and about two hundred were injured.

I will never forget seeing the live footage on the news as reports came in—and it hit me hard. Having worked in the business over twenty years at that point, I had been in countless venues like the Station to see bands at that level perform. Security and safety procedures were often lax at

ABOVE: Eddie and Jack Russell
RIGHT: Michael Lardie, Scott Snyder, Mark Kendall, and Terry Ilous
OPPOSITE: Jack Russell

those types of places, and though I had never been to the Station, seeing the people struggling to get out of the burning building was terrifying and sobering. Later, when I heard that the local radio DJ who hosted a metal show and had been on hand to MC also passed away, it hit even closer to home. Had it been a similar place in New York or New Jersey, that easily could have been me. Suddenly Great White was everywhere again, but for all the wrong reasons.

The next few years were emotionally charged as the investigation and legal process began. The whole thing was as sad and ugly as you could imagine. Jack Russell took to the road, donating money from all the gigs to the charity. But there wasn't much to donate. Even though his intentions were good, they weren't enough to get people out to see him play again—Jack's band was now damaged goods and the negative press was too hard to overcome. Other bands, like Twisted Sister, did successful benefits in the area for the families, but Jack and Great White weren't invited to be a part of them. Eventually, the tragedy, coupled with years of alcohol and drug abuse, caught up to him, and Jack was admitted to rehab. Everyone was pretty sure they had seen the end of Jack Russell and any version of Great White.

However, by 2007, enough wounds had healed and many of the raw emotions had subsided. Mark Kendall, Jack Russell, and the original Great White announced their intentions to reunite and began performing live again. I hosted several of these performances, and although Jack could still sing, he was dealing with a wide range of serious health issues, including a perforated bowel and back issues resulting from a fall. He often walked the stage with a cane, and there were even times he had to sit while he sang. As a result, Great White was forced to bring in replacement singers such as Jani Lane and Paul Shortino to get through their live performances. To me, Great White's strongest asset has always been Jack's voice, so it was all a bit of a mess to see a revolving door of band members replace him. But by 2011, Jack had finally pulled himself together, and I had him on *That Metal Show*. Even though he was frail, he was in good spirits, was moving well, and appeared sober and happy. Unfortunately, his Great White band members didn't wait around—they enlisted yet another new singer by the name of Terry Ilous, best known to rock fans as the singer in XYZ. This latest move hit Jack hard, and he retaliated by starting up his own Great White once again—contributing to a growing trend of there being two versions of a band touring and/or recording at the same time. Meanwhile, Great White released their debut with Ilous on vocals, titled *Elation*, in 2012.

In December 2012, I interviewed Mark Kendall and asked him if he saw any scenario where Great White would work again with their original voice. Emotions are still raw and legal issues are still in the courts, but Mark said anything was possible if Jack could prove his ability to stay sober. In the meantime, both versions of the band play Great White's catalog on an active touring schedule, and although Jack may still have his struggles, his voice is still very much with him.

GLENN HUGHES

Glenn Hughes is known simply as the "Voice of Rock" in his native England, and if you have ever heard the man sing, you know why. He is a stunning vocalist with a power, range, and soulfulness that is simply jaw-dropping, especially live. I will never forget asking the late, great Ronnie James Dio, who himself was rightfully regarded as one of rock's greatest singers, who his favorite singer was, and he answered immediately: Glenn Hughes. But, as with Deep Purple, one of the bands he is best known for being a member of, Glenn is tragically underrated and underappreciated in what is now his home country of the U.S.A. He is also a brilliant writer and bass player, but as noted producer Kevin Shirley rightfully said, so many talk about Glenn's astonishing vocal ability that often his playing is overlooked.

CLASSIC LINEUP:

GLENN HUGHES (BASS/VOCALS)

DISCOGRAPHY

SOLO:

PLAY ME OUT (1977)

SONGS IN THE KEY OF ROCK (2003)

SOUL MOVER (2005)

MUSIC FOR THE DIVINE (2006)

WITH TRAPEZE:

MEDUSA (1971)

WITH DEEP PURPLE:

BURN (1974)

STORMBRINGER (1974)

COME TASTE THE BAND (1975)

WITH PAT THRALL:

HUGHES/THRALL (1982)

WITH GARY MOORE:

RUN FOR COVER (1985)

WITH JOE LYNN TURNER:

HUGHES AND TURNER PROJECT (2002)

WITH TONY IOMMI:

FUSED (2005)

WITH

Glenn first came on the scene as the bassist in the early '70s band Trapeze. The band had a funky rock vibe that has been a Hughes signature ever since. It also included guitarist Mel Galley, who would later join Whitesnake, and drummer Dave Holland, who would later join Judas Priest and play on many of that band's classic albums. Trapeze built a solid following in Europe and certain parts of America, but not enough for Glenn to turn down an offer to join Deep Purple in 1973. Deep Purple's legendary Mark II lineup was disbanding, with vocalist Ian Gillan and bassist Roger Glover leaving. Glenn replaced Glover and the then-unknown David Coverdale took the frontman role from Gillan. Even though Coverdale was the primary lead singer in the new Mark III lineup, Deep Purple was in the unique position of having a bassist in Hughes who could sing equally well and, more important, in a different style. Where Coverdale had more of a raspy tone to his voice, Hughes could scream and hit highs unlike anything anybody had ever heard. As a result, many of the recordings Deep Purple made with this lineup also feature Glenn's voice prominently. I often wondered why Deep Purple didn't just make Glenn their singer at the time, but the thought was to have a dedicated frontman in Coverdale (who didn't play instruments live), backed by a powerhouse bassist/vocalist. Their voices also blended together beautifully.

Deep Purple, remarkably, remained a mega band after losing Glover and Gillan, two key members of their lineup. Much of the credit for that

ABOVE: Glenn Hughes
OPPOSITE: Eddie, Geezer Butler, and
Glenn Hughes

ABOVE: Eddie and Glenn Hughes

EDDIE'S PLAYLIST
GLENN HUGHES

1. THE GREAT DIVIDE (BLACK COUNTRY COMMUNION)
2. MUSCLE AND BLOOD (HUGHES/THRALL)
3. REACH FOR THE SKY (WITH GARY MOORE)
4. COAST TO COAST (TRAPEZE)
5. STEPPIN' ON
6. AFTERGLOW (BLACK COUNTRY COMMUNION)
7. NO STRANGER TO LOVE (WITH TONY IOMMI)
8. DOPAMINE (WITH TONY IOMMI)
9. MEDUSA (TRAPEZE)
10. SOUL MOVER

and Coverdale (and new guitarist Tommy Bolin), 1975's *Come Taste the Band*, was recorded with the Mark IV lineup, Glenn had gone off the deep end, and it was impacting his playing and performance. By 1976, Deep Purple was done. That same year, Bolin, who was one of Glenn's partying partners in Purple, lost his life to drugs. You would think this would scare Glenn straight, but it only fueled his addiction further.

What followed was a series of albums from Glenn, solo and with others. As much as the drugs had impaired him, people were still willing to bet on him—he was simply that talented. Glenn's huge passion for soul and funk was on prominent display on many of his solo recordings. The *Hughes/Thrall* album, made in 1982 with Pat Travers guitarist Pat Thrall, is regarded as a hard rock classic by many, but it failed to create major sales, and the pairing ended soon after the album was released. Next, guitarist Gary Moore, from Northern Ireland, enlisted Glenn to sing on several tracks for his 1985 album, *Run for Cover*. This also ended badly, because of Glenn's substance issues. But in a true testament to his talent, people kept thinking he would turn it around and kept knocking on his door. Black Sabbath guitarist and longtime friend Tony Iommi connected with Hughes in 1986 to sing on what was originally supposed to be an Iommi solo album but was released under the Sabbath name at the insistence of the record label. That album, *Seventh Star*, contains some great material, though it's not exactly Sabbath-sounding. Glenn often

ABOVE: Glenn Hughes

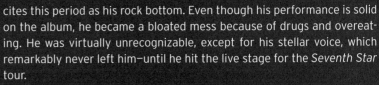

cites this period as his rock bottom. Even though his performance is solid on the album, he became a bloated mess because of drugs and overeating. He was virtually unrecognizable, except for his stellar voice, which remarkably never left him—until he hit the live stage for the *Seventh Star* tour.

It was bad enough that the Sabbath name was seriously diluted with a lineup that featured only Iommi from the original band, but making matters worse was Glenn, who could barely stand onstage, let alone sing. I attended one of the shows on this tour at the Meadowlands in New Jersey. Being naive about drug use, I was excited to hear songs from *Seventh Star* live. But Glenn literally had no ability to sing anymore. Instead of the awesome pipes that had been his trademark for so many years, he was reduced to a hoarse-sounding whisper, croaking out the lyrics. Sabbath knew trouble was brewing and had another singer waiting in the wings, a New Yorker by the name of Ray Gillen. Glenn saw Gillen around and thought he was a member of Anthrax, one of the opening bands on the tour, but Gillen was actually traveling with the band in preparation for replacing Glenn—which Gillen did just a few gigs later. It was at the Meadowlands show that things hit a breaking point. Glenn has told me many times this was a personal low for him and always feels he owes something extra to the people who paid for a ticket for that performance or lack thereof. The drugs had wrecked his vocal cords and blood was building in his throat—causing his voice to totally give out.

As talented as he was, Glenn was now considered a casualty of the music business, and his chances to come back were drying up. Yes, there were still albums and songs made, but he had become somewhat of a joke, defined more by his over-the-top drug use than his amazing musicianship, which had seemingly deserted him. It wasn't until the late '90s that Glenn finally got sober and became a changed man. The first album he made that truly announced he was back for real was 2005's *Soul Mover*. Teaming up with Chad Smith of the Red Hot Chili Peppers, Glenn found his funk-rock soul mate. (The album also features Chili Peppers ex-guitarists John Frusciante and Dave Navarro.) Remarkably, Glenn's voice came back to him, and a now-healthy Glenn was singing and playing as well as ever. It took a while for fans to believe it was for real this time, but Glenn hung in there and made a string of solid solo albums. I saw him headline a club show in New York City shortly after and took some friends who had no idea who Glenn was. They were absolutely floored by what they saw and heard that night coming from the man's voice. It was that good. Against all odds, Glenn Hughes was indeed back for good.

Over the years I have become friends with Glenn and have had him on my radio shows several times. I never knew Glenn Hughes as a drug addict; I have only known him personally as the sober Glenn, and one of the nicest and most loving people I've met—a man who truly realizes how lucky he is to be alive. When Ronnie James Dio passed away in 2010, Glenn and I spent a weekend together at three different services saying good-bye to our dear friend. Glenn sang a brilliant rendition of the Rainbow song "Catch the Rainbow" at the private funeral. I was so moved by it that I asked Ronnie's widow, Wendy, if Glenn could do it again at the public memorial I hosted. He did, and it was stunning. Around this same time, Glenn called me to tell me I would be very excited about his next project. He was pleased to be making a return to heavy rock once again with a new band called Black Country Communion. A supergroup of sorts, very much in the style of '70s Deep Purple, BCC also features guitarist Joe Bonamassa, keyboardist Derek Sherinian, and drummer Jason Bonham. BCC released their debut album in September 2010 and played live for the very first time on my satellite radio show. In two years, they have released three amazing albums and are without question one of my favorite newer bands because they are a group that totally channels the values of the old school: great playing, great songs, and amazing singing. Sadly, in 2013 BCC disbanded, but Glenn continues to work on his solo career as well as with a wide variety of artists. In 2011, Glenn released his autobiography, titled *Deep Purple and Beyond: Scenes from the Life of a Rock Star*. I was amazed at the stories in his book. It was as if I was reading about a totally different person—not the same man I now regard as a close friend—and as Glenn has told me, he was. I am such a fan of the music Glenn has given us over the decades, but I'm even more proud of the person he has become, and I enjoy our conversations and value our friendship. Long live the Voice of Rock!

UNDERGROUND CLASSIC

Check out Tony Iommi and Glenn Hughes's *The 1996 DEP Sessions*. This is an Iommi solo album that Glenn recorded the vocals for but that was later scrapped. The album was widely bootlegged, leading to an officially remixed and partially rerecorded release in 2005.

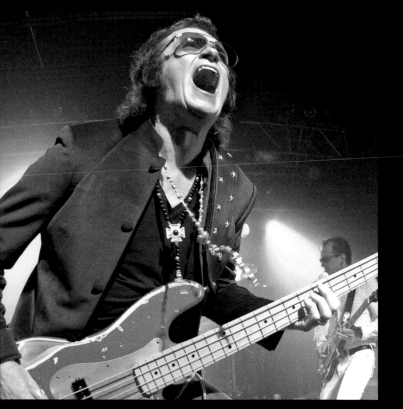

LEFT AND OPPOSITE: Glenn Hughes

KING'S X

After more than thirty years and countless incredible albums, King's X sadly remains somewhat of a cult phenomenon. I was working for Megaforce Records when the band's first demo came into our office. It was a video of drummer Jerry Gaskill, bassist Doug Pinnick, and guitarist Ty Tabor performing a song called "King" at a construction site. Label head Johnny Z sat me down and played the video, which was well done for an unsigned band that seemingly wouldn't have the resources to make a video. After we watched it, Johnny and I both looked at each other, neither of us entirely sure what we had just taken in, but also knowing that it was special. I remember sitting there with Johnny, trying to figure out if a metal label like Megaforce could actually break out a band like King's X. They fused gospel and bluesy vocals with hard rock wails and riffs. And the trio was anything but glamorous in an era of MTV pinups. But to Johnny's credit, he looked at me and said, "Ed, this is amazing. We have to go for it." I agreed, as did everyone else in our small office, and King's X was soon a Megaforce recording artist.

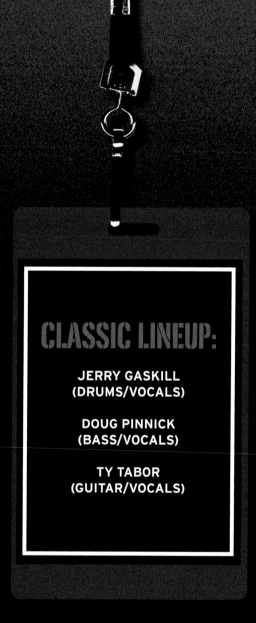

CLASSIC LINEUP:

JERRY GASKILL
(DRUMS/VOCALS)

DOUG PINNICK
(BASS/VOCALS)

TY TABOR
(GUITAR/VOCALS)

OPPOSITE: Jerry Gaskill, Doug Pinnick, and Ty Tabor

DISCOGRAPHY

OUT OF THE SILENT PLANET
(1988)

*GRETCHEN GOES
TO NEBRASKA* (1989)

FAITH HOPE LOVE (1990)

KING'S X (1992)

DOGMAN (1994)

EAR CANDY (1996)

TAPE HEAD (1998)

*PLEASE COME
HOME . . . MR. BULBOUS*
(2000)

MANIC MOONLIGHT (2001)

BLACK LIKE SUNDAY
(2003)

OGRE TONES (2005)

XV (2008)

A few short weeks later, the three members of King's X, along with their producer and manager, Sam Taylor, joined us at Johnny and Marsha Z's home in New Jersey (which was, at the time, also doubling as the label's office) for a backyard barbecue to celebrate signing them to the label. I wasn't surprised to see Sam sticking close to the band. The impact that Sam Taylor had on King's X at this time can't be stressed enough. He was extremely knowledgeable about the business, having worked for a company that managed ZZ Top. He was, in fact, so involved in the band's career that he was basically the fourth member. Sam managed the band's affairs, produced their records, directed their videos, and even played a few things on the album. He was a nice enough guy to deal with, but some felt that his involvement on the creative end could occasionally be too controlling. Sam had a vision for the band—but it was very different from what was happening at the time in popular music.

The trio had been slugging it out for quite a while before they signed with Megaforce. The band's history dates back to 1979, when Doug Pinnick and Jerry Gaskill were working together in Springfield, Missouri, with various musicians and Christian rock bands. After moving around a bit, they met Ty Tabor and eventually settled in Houston, Texas, where they met Sam Taylor, who suggested they change their name from Sneak Preview to King's X. Nine years after Doug and Jerry first got together, the King's X debut album, *Out of the Silent Planet*, was released on Megaforce Records.

Everyone at Megaforce was blown away by the sound these three guys created, mixing incredible guitar and three-part vocal harmonies into an almost psychedelic stew. At their best, they were a hard rock Beatles who presented a soulful sound rarely heard in hard rock music. They pushed themselves to combine many musical genres—R&B and funk with hard rock and metal—and they weren't afraid to jam. We were all excited by the possibility that they could have crossover potential to reach new audiences and take the label to a new level. Sadly, that never happened. The truth of the matter is that audiences didn't know quite what to make of them. Their talent as musicians and writers was undeniable to anyone who heard them, but they didn't quite mesh with the hard rock of the era. Most King's X records took you on a musical journey that you needed a few listens to really absorb, because of their many musical influences and their experimental nature. Sam's production also didn't have the pop of other albums of the day, their look wasn't what was happening at the time, and there were Christian rock and literary overtones to their music and imagery that alienated some listeners. Radio was resistant to the band, to say the least.

Deep down, I knew that King's X was an amazing band, but I also knew that a metal label with a small staff and without huge marketing money didn't stand a chance of surmounting this rising tide of issues. But everyone tried their hardest. What kept us fighting was not only the greatness of the band but also the positive response from the critics and fans who *did* get it. Reviews for *Out of the Silent Planet* were strong, and other

musicians from major bands fell in love with King's X—resulting in some pretty cool live gigs. (For example, getting the call to tour with Pearl Jam.) I joked at the time that if promotional copies counted toward album sales, the band would have gone platinum! Everyone in the industry would call the office for a promo of the latest King's X album, but sadly not nearly as many copies crossed record store counters. Because there was so much industry buzz, there was the misconception that King's X was a much bigger success than they ever were. People are stunned when I tell them that King's X never even scored a gold album in America. Megaforce believed in them like no other artist on the label's roster at the time, but it just never translated to sales.

Gretchen Goes to Nebraska, released in 1989, is regarded by many as the classic King's X album, highlighted by the track "Over My Head," which was the closest they ever got to truly cracking radio and scoring some MTV play. Back then, MTV had a countdown request show, and Megaforce, along with our distributing label, Atlantic, would recruit kids to jam the call-in line so the King's X video would show up in the countdown (a common thing for many labels to do at the time). Faith Hope Love followed in 1990 and received more buzz, with more touring, and even some limited radio and video play. But for their next album, King's X switched to Atlantic Records and severed ties with Sam Taylor. Sam was the band's biggest believer for many years, but he didn't always make the decisions that might have allowed them to sell more records and broaden their audience. The band was hoping a new perspective would finally put them over the top.

But even with a new label—complete with new producers and managers—King's X never got the huge breakthrough they deserved. Now, don't

UNDERGROUND CLASSIC

All the members of King's X have recorded solo work. In 2012, Doug Pinnick sang guest vocals on a cover of the Dokken song "Tooth and Nail" with a band named T&N, featuring former Dokken members. This led to one of many new projects he is launching with former Dokken guitarist George Lynch.

ABOVE: Ty Tabor, Doug Pinnick, and Jerry Gaskill
OPPOSITE: Ty Tabor, Doug Pinnick, Eddie, and Jerry Gaskill

EDDIE'S PLAYLIST

KING'S X

1. POWER OF LOVE
2. SUMMERLAND
3. FOOL YOU
4. IT'S LOVE
5. VISIONS

6. OVER MY HEAD
7. MOANJAM
8. DOGMAN
9. GOLDILOX
10. PRAY

get me wrong—the band's story certainly has some high points, like great touring opportunities opening for giants like AC/DC and Robert Plant, to name a few. Their music appeared in the 1991 film *Bill and Ted's Bogus Journey*, they played Woodstock in 1994, and they carved out an incredibly passionate fan base. Simply put, it's been thirty years and they are still in it for all the right reasons, playing music from the heart. This longevity has also afforded the band members opportunities to pursue solo projects and to spread out from time to time. All of that said, it still continues to be incredibly frustrating for many fans that King's X never hit it big. But to the band's credit, they have never given up. They continue as the original trio.

King's X wrote a song called "Go Tell Somebody" on their 2008 album, *XV*, encouraging fans to, if they liked what they were hearing, "go tell somebody." So I hope that's what I'm doing right now with this chapter! I have a tremendous amount of respect for King's X. Few bands have come up with a sound as unique and continue to have a huge impact on the many fans and musicians who discover them—plus, they're just good people and great musicians. I recently spent some time in L.A. with Doug, who is now in his sixties and as exuberant about making music as he was when I first met him at that Megaforce barbecue. So, go tell somebody! It's never too late!

LEFT: Doug Pinnick and Ty Tabor
OPPOSITE TOP: Ty Tabor
OPPOSITE BOTTOM: Jerry Gaskill

YNGWIE MALMSTEEN

Yngwie Malmsteen first came on my radar with the Los Angeles band Steeler back in 1982. People could barely pronounce his name properly, but everyone was talking about him. Not since Eddie Van Halen were so many people impacted by a guitar player. Malmsteen's mix of neoclassical and hard rock, coupled with blazing speed, became the toast of the rock and metal world almost immediately after his arrival from Sweden. He was first inspired to pick up a guitar after seeing Jimi Hendrix burn one on TV, and he was influenced by Ritchie Blackmore and Uli Jon Roth, as well as classical composers, resulting in his unique approach to the instrument.

CLASSIC LINEUP:

YNGWIE MALMSTEEN (GUITAR)

OPPOSITE: Yngwie Malmsteen

DID YOU KNOW

Yngwie now lives in Miami with his family. His wife, April, serves as his manager. His birth name is Lars Johann Yngve Lannerbäck. Malmsteen is Yngwie's mother's maiden name.

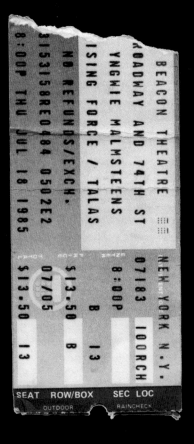

Yngwie's gateway to America was Mike Varney, a San Francisco Bay Area producer, writer, and label executive who had a knack for discovering and nurturing up-and-coming players. Varney's label, Shrapnel, was and continues to be, a breaking ground for some of the best players to emerge in rock and metal. At the time, Steeler consisted of drummer Mark Edwards, bassist Rik Fox, and vocalist Ron Keel (who later had some success with his namesake band, Keel). They had recently parted ways with their guitarist when Varney suggested Malmsteen and essentially plugged him into the band. Steeler's material for its first, self-titled album had been largely written and was simply in need of the guitar parts when Yngwie was presented with it. And the guitar tracks he recorded were the world's introduction to one of music's most accomplished players of all time.

I've spoken with Yngwie many times about this period, and although he acknowledges Steeler's importance, he considers it his version of elementary school—a nice start, but he always had bigger plans. He recorded all the guitar solos on the album in roughly a day. Once Varney released Steeler, word spread quickly—not so much about the band or the songs but about the guy from Sweden shredding guitar solos at the speed of light. And it became a top-selling independent album, one that's still in demand to this day. I certainly don't want to discount the contributions of the other members of Steeler—there are some good songs and performances—but take it from a kid working in a record store when the album came out: Everyone wanted it because of Yngwie.

DISCOGRAPHY

RISING FORCE (1984)

MARCHING OUT (1985)

TRILOGY (1986)

ODYSSEY (1988)

ECLIPSE (1990)

FIRE AND ICE (1992)

I CAN'T WAIT EP (1994)

THE SEVENTH SIGN (1994)

MAGNUM OPUS (1995)

INSPIRATION (1996)

FACING THE ANIMAL (1997)

CONCERTO SUITE FOR
ELECTRIC GUITAR
AND ORCHESTRA IN
E FLAT MINOR, OPUS 1 (1998)

ALCHEMY (1999)

WAR TO END ALL WARS
(2000)

UNLEASH THE FURY (2005)

PERPETUAL FLAME (2008)

RELENTLESS (2010)

SPELLBOUND (2012)

After the one album with Steeler, Yngwie was courted by several artists, and major bands like Kiss and UFO even sniffed around to gauge his interest in joining them. But his next stop was in a group called Alcatrazz, fronted by former Rainbow singer Graham Bonnet and with bassist Gary Shea and keyboardist Jimmy Waldo, both former members of the '70s band New England (I was a big fan). Drummer Jan Uvena rounded out the lineup. Malmsteen told me that he had turned down invitations from major established bands at the time because he wasn't interested in filling someone else's shoes or playing other guitarists' material. He wanted to write and create new music, and with Alcatrazz he was part of something from the ground floor. Even though he seemed to have the band he was looking for, Yngwie made only one studio and one live album with Alcatrazz before leaving for his inevitable solo career. (Steve Vai replaced him for Alcatrazz's next studio album, *Disturbing the Peace*.)

It was clear that Yngwie was going to be the star of any band he was a part of and that solo albums were what his fans were hoping for. These albums showcase him not only as a brilliant player but also as the writer of all of his music and the captain of the ship. Because of his huge interest in classical music and his prolific career, he has been able to make a vast number of albums of differing styles—heavy rock, metal, or more melodic material, with or without singers, with or without an orchestra. For me, his career-defining albums are his earliest solo recordings: 1984's *Rising Force* (which was nominated for a Grammy) and 1985's *Marching*

TOP: Yngwie Malmsteen
BOTTOM: Yngwie Malmsteen and Eddie
OPPOSITE: Yngwie Malmsteen

UNDERGROUND CLASSIC

Check out the 1999 cover of Aerosmith's "Dream On" done by Yngwie and Ronnie James Dio. It was originally recorded for a tribute album and since has turned up on various compilations.

Out, both featuring the vocals of Jeff Scott Soto. These albums contain the perfect balance of great hard rock guitar and vocals.

Yngwie's biggest commercial breakthrough came in 1988 with his fourth solo release, Odyssey, which features former Rainbow singer Joe Lynn Turner as well as former Ozzy Osbourne bassist and songwriter Bob Daisley. "Heaven Tonight" remains Malmsteen's most hook-filled single from this album and came the closest to being a mainstream hit. But despite his numerous solo albums highlighting his virtuosic technique, Malmsteen waned in popularity in the '90s, perhaps because of changing times and a reduced focus on shredding guitar solos, or perhaps because his playing style began to seem repetitive to some fans. Still, countless guitarists owe a huge debt to Yngwie, whose guitar playing they've no doubt spent countless hours trying to imitate.

Any discussion of Yngwie Malmsteen would not be complete without mentioning the man's ego. You see, for a long time, stories of Yngwie's personality were almost as notorious as those about his masterful playing. He has a reputation as an egomaniac and control freak, which he fully admitted to being when I had him on That Metal Show. One of my favorite Yngwie stories happened back in 2000 in the studio of my radio show when it was on WNEW in New York—the first time I had Malmsteen in the studio in person. He has used the words "Yngwie J. Malmsteen's Rising Force" on his albums, which led me to think that "Rising Force" was what he called his band. So innocently enough, I asked Yngwie, "Who's in Rising Force with you these days?" He looked at me and seemed upset. "Rising Force? Rising Force? Why would you ask me about Rising Force? There is no Rising Force. Nobody cares about that. There is only YNGWIE!" It was then that I realized the rap on Yngwie was very real. But we still had a great talk and have done many interviews over the years.

In 2008 I booked Yngwie as a guest in my first season of That Metal Show. To his credit, he flew himself in and out of New York just to do the show when it was in its infancy, and he was great. I saw some real change in him now that he was older. He was more mature and willing to compromise. Yngwie arrived at the TMS taping with his guitar in tow, so we thought it might be cool for him to play some licks into the commercial breaks. Our show's soundman had set a small amp in the corner, along with a mic that was placed maybe twelve inches from the amp. Yngwie got up, looked at the mic, moved it maybe six inches closer to the amp, and then sat down on the set. Minutes later, the soundman emerged, looked at the mic, shook his head, and pulled it back to twelve inches. This uncomfortable exchange happened about four times, and I could see tensions brewing on both sides. So I stepped in to mediate. The sound guy tried to explain to Yngwie that he'd specifically set the mic up there to get the best guitar sound for the TV mix. I could feel a classic Malmsteen meltdown coming, but to my great surprise and relief, Yngwie took a deep breath, shrugged his shoulders, said something like "Whatever works," and sat back down! I was stunned. People still talk about that show, and later I questioned Yngwie about what seemed like a new willingness to bend a bit when working with other people. He admitted that his wife, April, had talked with him and was trying to help him become a slightly kinder, gentler, more adaptable Yngwie. I've since had him on the TV show twice, and I always get a kick out of him and respect where he is coming from. Most recently, he has been making records with former Judas Priest singer Tim "Ripper" Owens, and they are much harder than anything he has done in a while. However, regardless of who he has surrounding him, as history has shown time and time again, anything Yngwie puts out is truly all about Yngwie!

ABOVE: Yngwie Malmsteen

MANOWAR

Perhaps no band lives and breathes all things metal like Manowar. When they came on the scene in the early '80s, Manowar embodied metal like no other group. Many people find it easy to look at them and write them off as a silly bunch of guys who think they are Vikings or cavemen, clad in their leather and animal skins. However, they are missing out on some of the best power metal ever made. Manowar's style is no contrived image. Their image simply brings their music—their dark, epic songs filled with tales of fantasy, violence, and death and with heavy riffs and melodies—to life.

CLASSIC LINEUP:

ERIC ADAMS (VOCALS)

JOEY DEMAIO (BASS)

ROSS "THE BOSS" FRIEDMAN (GUITAR)

DONNIE HAMZIK (DRUMS)

KEY ADDITIONAL MEMBERS:

SCOTT COLUMBUS (DRUMS)

RHINO EDWARDS (DRUMS)

KARL LOGAN (GUITAR)

DAVID SHANKLE (GUITAR)

DISCOGRAPHY

Bassist Joey DeMaio formed Manowar with guitarist Ross "the Boss" Friedman when the two met on Black Sabbath's *Heaven and Hell* tour in 1980. Joey was working as a bass tech for Sabbath, and Ross–a former member of New York City legends the Dictators–was playing in the opening act Shakin' Street. Years later Joey told me that being out there on the road for Sabbath's first tour with Ronnie James Dio had had a huge impact on him. Joey was a fan of Dio's (both were from upstate New York) and admired his approach to his music as well as the way he conducted himself. And Joey credits his friendship with Ronnie as playing a key role in inspiring him to form Manowar. After spending a good deal of time together on the road with Sabbath, Ross and Joey decided to start a band once the tour ended. They recruited singer Eric Adams, a friend of DeMaio's, and drummer Carl Canedy, from the band the Rods, to play on the demo that led to a deal with Liberty Records. Soon after, they released their debut and all-time classic album, *Battle Hymns*, by which time drummer Donnie Hamzik had joined the band. (Canedy, after spending so much time on the road, decided to focus on a career in producing.)

This incredible first onslaught of Manowar was unlike anything anyone had heard in metal up to that point. *Battle Hymns* predated the debut of the thrash scene by a year or more, and I see it as an important bridge to that sound. Not so much in its speed–a signature of thrash–but in its sheer, uncompromising power and heaviness. The album has just eight tracks, and they made each one count, with stellar production, playing, and vocals from the incomparable Eric Adams. Famed actor Orson Welles even has a guest role as a narrator on the epic track "Dark Avenger."

Manowar began to tour internationally following the success of *Battle Hymns* and quickly established one of their trademark styles: playing shows at a deafening volume. As a matter of fact, they made the *Guinness Book of World Records* in 1984 for the loudest performance ever–and have twice since beaten their own record! My ears would ring for days after seeing them live. I remember going to a Manowar show at a New Jersey club called Obsessions with my friend D.D. Verni from Overkill, who is a huge Manowar fan. The club had a glass wall separating the bar for those of legal drinking age from the area for the fans who were under twenty-one. I swear, there were moments when I thought the glass was going to shatter from the volume as DeMaio's bass rumbled the walls!

Almost from the beginning, Manowar had a no-compromise, take-no-prisoners approach to their live gigs. They bled power and confidence with every note, and the world took quick notice. This intense passion and commitment saw the band build an incredibly loyal fan base with subsequent albums *Into Glory Ride* in 1983 and their most successful release, 1988's *Kings of Metal*, with classics like the title track and "Hail and Kill" (these became staples in Manowar's sets). Their audience continued to grow each year, and after several independent record deals, the group was signed to Atlantic Records, then Geffen. This was no small feat when you consider that even though Manowar had a rabid fan base in the '80s and early '90s, they had nowhere near as much radio success–something

DID YOU KNOW ?

Manowar makes their own amps and guitars, and were also one of the first metal bands to feature orchestration in their music.

most major labels required of the bands they signed in those days. A few of Manowar's great metal anthems almost crossed into commercial territory, such as "Fighting the World" and "Blow Your Speakers," but both fell short of taking the band to massive heights in the United States.

However, what Manowar lacked in U.S. mass-market appeal, they more than made up for in Europe and other parts of the world. European audiences seemed to really *get* them. The love of the mythology behind their songs and image, the huge Viking choruses, and the extreme volume of their playing resonated, making Manowar regulars on the international festival circuit. While the band had always been able to pack a night or two in American clubs or small theaters, in countries like Greece, England, and Germany, to name a few, they could headline festivals. I think European audiences really appreciate Manowar's unwillingness to compromise on how they do things, sometimes at the expense of gaining further exposure. And as a result, they have an incredibly loyal fan base known as "Manowarriors."

Once DeMaio got a taste of the size of European audiences and the scope of the shows his band could deliver with the resources available overseas, Manowar reduced the number of shows they performed on their home soil. (Joey has invited me many times to witness their shows in Europe, and one day I hope to join them.) It became harder and harder to justify playing clubs in the United States for sleazy promoters with subpar PA systems when they could be headlining festivals elsewhere in the world. To this day, the band plays only three to five U.S. shows a year, if any, making them true destination events for their American fans. Joey is meticulous about the band's live sound, and if the house PA isn't loud enough, Manowar has been known to bring in their own! They're not loud just for the sake of being loud; the sound has to be balanced and mixed to a precise level of pure, clean, and clear volume, never distorted. I've watched the band's soundcheck, and while many groups will just run through a song or two to work out kinks in the PA system, Manowar's

LEFT: Joey DeMaio, Eric Adams, and Karl Logan
ABOVE: Joey DeMaio
OPPOSITE: Eric Adams

EDDIE'S PLAYLIST
MANOWAR

1. WARRIORS OF THE WORLD
2. BLOW YOUR SPEAKERS
3. KILL WITH POWER
4. METAL DAZE
5. DEFENDER
6. MANOWAR
7. WARLORD
8. BLACK WIND, FIRE AND STEEL
9. BATTLE HYMN
10. FIGHTING THE WORLD

soundchecks are as detailed as the actual performance later that night, with Joey often walking around the venue, checking to make sure every corner is fully saturated with glorious metal excess!

Manowar, though, is more than just volume. The amazing vocals of Eric Adams are key. His range, with his powerful wails, is simply stunning, and he is tragically overlooked in the discussion of the great metal singers of all time. Much of the successful early material and the band's direction were guided by founding members DeMaio, clearly the band's leader, and Ross the Boss, who wrote the bulk of the songs. However, as a series of lineup changes took place—first, Hamzik was replaced by Scott Columbus, and then Ross left in 1988 and was replaced by David Shankle and later by current guitarist Karl Logan—DeMaio was left in a position to fully take control of all aspects of the band. He writes all of the band's material, does the bulk of the press, produces the albums, and even started his own production company, called Magic Circle Music, which handles all affairs for the band and has launched the careers of a few others.

Manowar has continued to go strong throughout the years, and in 2002 released what is one of my favorite later Manowar albums, *Warriors of the World*. The album embodies the great metal spirit that is Manowar, and its title track is an anthem for the band's global fan base. It also features strong production and a good selection of the different styles of metal that Manowar is so good at—incorporating classic influences while painting their songs with a very epic brush! In 2011 the band celebrated their landmark debut, *Battle Hymns,* by totally rerecording the album, throwing in some different arrangements, and rereleasing it as a special edition. That recording marked the return of original drummer Donnie Hamzik as a replacement for Scott Columbus, who had passed away that same year. It's amazing to think that after being out of the band for nearly thirty years, Hamzik returned to the fold full-time by rerecording the same Manowar album he started with!

In 2012 Manowar released *The Lord of Steel*, featuring the tracks "El Gringo," which was created for a film of the same name, and "Expendable," made for the Sylvester Stallone action film *The Expendables 2*. Over the years, I've always enjoyed talking with Joey DeMaio—you gotta love someone so dedicated to metal and his craft. Joey told me he was able to play "Expendable" for Stallone personally and enjoyed seeing the Hollywood legend bang his head to the sounds of Manowar! Fiercely proud of the music they have made over the decades, their loyal fan base, and what they stand for in metal, Manowar is the real deal.

UNDERGROUND CLASSIC

Ross the Boss released a power pop album with a band called the Spina-tras in 1999 titled *@Midnight.com*. A far cry from the metal of Manowar, it's still good melodic rock.

ABOVE: Joey DeMaio
OPPOSITE: Ross "the Boss" Friedman

MARILYN MANSON

My first exposure to Marilyn Manson came when the debut CD *Portrait of an American Family* arrived at my radio show at WDHA in New Jersey. The mid-'90s weren't a great time for new music for me. The grunge movement was in full swing, and every band sounded like they were from Seattle, even if they weren't. It wasn't about being a rock star; it was about being an anti-rock star. And as a fan of the great bands of the '70s and '80s, I wasn't into it. I liked Soundgarden and Alice in Chains, and even a little of Pearl Jam, but I hated that every new band felt like a copycat and that the media seemed to cast out anything that wasn't deemed alternative. So I was pleasantly surprised when I listened to the Marilyn Manson debut. Here was a band that had a big live show and an image, and they sure as hell weren't grunge! (Can you imagine Marilyn Manson in flannel?) The band members had names like Madonna Wayne Gacy, Twiggy Ramirez, Ginger Fish, and of course the leader, Mr. Manson himself. The album was

CLASSIC LINEUP:

GINGER FISH (DRUMS)

MADONNA WAYNE GACY (KEYBOARDS)

JOHN 5 (GUITAR)

MARILYN MANSON (VOCALS)

TWIGGY RAMIREZ (BASS)

KEY ADDITIONAL MEMBERS:

DAISY BERKOWITZ (GUITAR)

SARA LEE LUCAS (DRUMS)

TIM SKÖLD (BASS)

DISCOGRAPHY

produced by Trent Reznor of Nine Inch Nails, who released it on his own label, Nothing Records. There was a bit of an industrial sound, but there were also heavy, dark riffs that showed a metal influence. It was unique, fresh, and exciting at a time when I thought most new music was redundant. I immediately became a Manson fan.

The reaction to my playing songs like "Lunchbox" and "Get Your Gunn" from that debut on my radio shows was mixed. My audience preferred more traditional metal for the most part, but even though Marilyn Manson's music might have been slightly outside the norm, I wanted to support what they were doing. I went to see the band live for the first time shortly after *Portrait* was released, and it was one of the most intense, dangerous shows I've ever seen. It was at a now-defunct club in Old Bridge, New Jersey, called Birch Hill. Maybe three hundred to four hundred people turned out to see them—respectable for a new band on a weeknight, but the club was far from packed. The band was new to many outside their native Florida, where they had worked the club scene under the name Marilyn Manson and the Spooky Kids. They wore makeup that made them look demented, bass player Twiggy Ramirez wore a dress, keyboardist Madonna Wayne Gacy jumped around like he was possessed, and before the show started, a road crew member warned the crowd that if they dared to come onstage during the performance, the band reserved the right to do physical harm against trespassers. I had never seen a band threaten bodily harm to their fans! But it didn't seem like an act at all. Manson was wild onstage—gyrating, spitting, cutting himself, and hitting his band members. And true to their word, when stage divers got onstage, they had the shit kicked out of them by the band or crew. Fans took the base of Manson's mic stand to the ribs, and they were dragged out the side door and thrown into the parking lot. For real! But everyone loved it, even the bloodied fans who managed to sneak back in after being disposed of. It was like a rock car crash—you wanted to look away, but you just couldn't help yourself.

I went to the radio station the next day and told everyone about my new favorite band, and word started to spread nationally. I called the label and asked to get an interview with Manson. I had to hear this guy speak and see what his deal was. Was he the crazed devil worshipper I had read about? Or was he more like Gene Simmons—an astute businessman who was executing a genius marketing plan? To be honest, after what I saw at Birch Hill, I was a little apprehensive to have Manson on my show; I just didn't know what I would be dealing with. The band agreed to come into my studio after a gig in New York, but it was canceled at the last minute when their bus broke down. It wouldn't be until years later that I would interview Manson, but they had a new fan either way.

In 1995 the band released the EP *Smells like Children* and scored a huge hit with their cover of the Eurythmics' "Sweet Dreams." The EP went gold, and suddenly Manson was a household name, with a huge following of both alternative rock fans and goth-leaning metalheads. Large numbers of kids were turning up at the shows dressed like their favorite band

member, and many goth girls were following the band around, at times looking more bizarre than Manson himself!

Most fans consider the band's second full-length album, *Antichrist Superstar*, their best. It's a huge step forward in production, with a more industrial sound tied together with conceptual pieces and Manson's equally haunting (and at times screaming) vocal delivery. I don't like it as much as their debut, but over the years it has grown on me. Some of the stuff is among the heaviest they have ever recorded, like the title track, "Irresponsible Hate Anthem," and the breakthrough hit "The Beautiful People." As the band became bigger and bigger, they put more money into the live show, and it became a true spectacle. In about a year and a half, they went from being this little band from Florida that nobody had

LEFT: Marilyn Manson
OPPOSITE: Twiggy Ramirez

EDDIE'S PLAYLIST

MARILYN MANSON

1. GREAT BIG WHITE WORLD
2. MECHANICAL ANIMALS
3. THE LOVE SONG
4. NO REFLECTION
5. MOBSCENE
6. ANTICHRIST SUPERSTAR
7. THE FIGHT SONG
8. GET YOUR GUNN
9. COMA WHITE
10. LUNCHBOX

heard of to headlining the Roseland in New York City for about four thousand people. Manson mania was in full swing, complete with controversy from religious groups that believed he was the devil. This was reinforced by Manson's own proclamation that he was a practicing satanist and anointed by Anton LaVey in the Church of Satan.

Album number three for the band remains my favorite to this day. *Mechanical Animals* shows what is regarded as Manson's "David Bowie phase." It's more melodic and glam influenced, with brilliant production. "Coma White," "Great Big White World," "Mechanical Animals," and "Rock Is Dead" are some of my favorite songs in the band's catalog. Guitarist John 5 joined the band for the album *Holy Wood* in 2000. Another monster album, it walked the line between the more hooky elements of *Mechanical Animals* and the heaviness of *Antichrist Superstar*. It also continued the band's trademark of incredibly cool production—great mixes, layers of weird sounds, conceptual elements that blended songs together—along with creepy cover images and packaging.

The remaining albums in the catalog are uneven to me. All have moments I like, but none offer the complete experience that the first few releases deliver. I was a fan of the album *Eat Me, Drink Me* in 2007, but most fans had fallen by the wayside. By this point, Manson himself was living the celebrity life and partying too hard, and it impacted his focus.

He married and dated Hollywood starlets, began painting and directing, and was drinking and drugging a lot. It bothers me to this day that just about every interview I read with Manson was about anything but music, the thing I most liked about him. I finally had Manson on my radio show in a phone interview for *Holy Wood*. By now I had seen and read much about him and knew he was a very smart guy, and also very funny. He certainly believed in what he was doing, and it wasn't all an act, but there was a bit of tongue-in-cheek in there, too.

Manson eluded me when we started doing *That Metal Show* in 2008. I wanted him on the show badly, but the timing just never worked out. Finally I managed to get him booked in 2011. He shared the show with Biff Byford of Saxon, who came on second. Manson arrived at the studio hammered on his drink of choice, absinthe, which is known to have hallucino-

LEFT: Marilyn Manson
OPPOSITE TOP AND BOTTOM:
Twiggy Ramirez

genic qualities. The form of it he drinks (along with God knows what else!) is actually illegal in the United States and is imported from Germany. He was tuned up on the stuff when we filmed that day, and if you saw the episode, you know I even had a sip with him. Manson was all over the map in the interview, saying wildly offensive stuff and living up to the shock-rocker image he prides himself on. It was hard to keep the interview on track. I felt bad for Biff, but knew exactly what I had gotten us into. If you want a straight, politically correct interview, you don't book a guy who calls himself "the God of Fuck." That episode of *That Metal Show* was the most heavily edited for language and content in the show's history. Even after all the editing, there were many who found it objectionable. It is without a doubt the most polarizing *TMS* episode ever. I received hate mail for having him on, along with praise for riveting television—in a nutshell, that *is* the story of Marilyn Manson. As his stage name reflects, he embodies both beauty and evil and our society's fascination with both.

In 2012 Manson released his most complete studio album in years, *Born Villain*. Written and produced largely by Manson and Twiggy, who came back to the band after years away, it's a return to that great balance of melody and heaviness. I went to see the band live in New Jersey when the album came out, and after the show I went into Manson's dressing room to say hi. As you might expect, it's very cold and very dark in there.

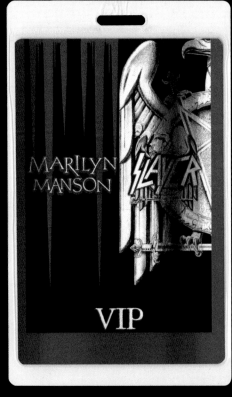

Manson held court with me and my friends for a couple of hours, playing a wildly random mix of music from his iPod, telling hysterical stories, and playing a game of naming obscure bands, which continued via text message after I left. Soon after, I went to see him in New York City co-headlining with Rob Zombie on a tour called Twins of Evil. This time, Manson plugged in my iPod and sang karaoke to obscure Kiss songs from *Unmasked*. He acknowledges the huge impact bands like Kiss (his first concert, in 1979), Alice Cooper, and others had on him growing up, and Manson is a true music fan of many styles of rock.

It is never dull around Marilyn Manson. Sure, he pushes the boundaries at times and can be offensive, controversial, and over-the-top. But we need more rock stars in this world, and I wouldn't have it any other way.

LEFT: Daisy Berkowitz
ABOVE: Eddie and Marilyn Manson
OPPOSITE TOP LEFT: Marilyn Manson
OPPOSITE TOP RIGHT: John 5
OPPOSITE BOTTOM: Twiggy Ramirez

NIGHT RANGER

I vividly recall seeing Night Ranger for the first time on MTV. The channel was new at the time, and very few houses had it. It was 1982, I was about to graduate high school, and I had no long-term goals except for continuing to pursue my love of hard rock music and seeing where it could take me. Many nights I would drive to a friend's house three towns away to sit there all night and watch MTV, hoping to see videos from bands we loved or to discover new music. When MTV played a video by Night Ranger for a song called "Don't Tell Me You Love Me," I was immediately interested in this new hard rock band. Bassist Jack Blades was bouncing around full of energy and singing lead vocals, and there were two incredibly blazing lead guitarists in Brad Gillis and Jeff Watson. The song was hard rocking and kicked ass! Drummer Kelly Keagy had positioned his kit sideways and also sang lead vocals, making for some great harmonies. (He positioned his kit this way so he would have a clear view of the crowd when singing.) Night Ranger had an ability and a confidence that seemed unusual for a new band, and they sold it well in the video. I've always loved melodic hard rock with great vocals and guitar playing, and Night Ranger had it in spades.

CLASSIC LINEUP:

JACK BLADES
(BASS/VOCALS)

ALAN FITZGERALD
(KEYBOARDS)

BRAD GILLIS (GUITAR)

KELLY KEAGY
(DRUMS/VOCALS)

JEFF WATSON (GUITAR)

KEY ADDITIONAL MEMBERS:

REB BEACH (GUITAR)

JOEL HOEKSTRA (GUITAR)

GARY MOON
(BASS/VOCALS)

OPPOSITE: Joel Hoekstra, Jack Blades, and Brad Gillis

DISCOGRAPHY

It turned out that one of the reasons the band seemed so seasoned right out of the gate was that even though Night Ranger was a new band of sorts, many of its members had a good deal of experience before they came together in San Francisco. Brad Gillis and Jack Blades were members of a pop funk band called Rubicon in the late '70s, while keyboardist Alan "Fitz" Fitzgerald played with Montrose and others. Of most note to metal fans was guitarist Brad Gillis, who had the daunting task of being the first real guitarist Ozzy Osbourne took under his wing after the tragic death of Randy Rhoads (with respect to Bernie Tormé, whom Brad replaced after Bernie had been in Ozzy's band for a handful of gigs and who was by everyone's account not the right fit). Brad had been working on Night Ranger while also playing in a Bay Area cover band called Alameda All Stars when he got the audition and eventual job in Ozzy's band. It was a tough gig to walk into, not only because of the level of Rhoads's playing but also because Brad was the first guitarist Ozzy introduced as a replacement for one of the most loved players in rock. Brad told me that many nights he would look out in the crowd to a sea of middle fingers pointing at him from fans mourning the loss of Randy. That never quite made sense to me. I know Randy was a legend, but Brad had nothing to do with his death and Ozzy chose to continue playing music, so somebody had to take the slot! Brad recorded the live Ozzy album *Speak of the Devil* but never recorded a studio album of new material with Ozzy. Eventually fans accepted him, but Brad decided to leave the band in 1982, after a year of touring, because he had made a commitment to his friends back home to see Night Ranger through. A ballsy move if you think about it. Here was a guy who had a major gig as a star player with a legend like

Ozzy but decided to roll the dice with his buddies in a band that might not ever make it. Even though the decision was tough, Brad knew that, with Ozzy, he would always be the guy who had replaced Randy, and creatively, it would be more fulfilling to play material he wrote and be a part of something new.

Night Ranger's debut album, *Dawn Patrol*, was released in 1982 and went on to score a modest rock hit with "Don't Tell Me You Love Me." The album sold well enough to establish the band with rock fans and get them touring, which is where they were always their best. I saw Night Ranger live for the first time very early on, and it reaffirmed the feeling I had when I had watched the video that day at my friend's house: They were a killer hard rock band. Live, Night Ranger had a tremendous amount of energy. The combined vocals of Jack and Kelly were stellar, with big harmonies, and Brad and Jeff were two of the best players I had ever seen in one band. Most two-guitar bands are built on the formula of a stud lead player and a supporting guitarist playing rhythm and the occasional lead. But Night Ranger had two equally amazing players who had different styles that also could mesh together for harmony lead guitar work. I always call Brad the "King of the Whammy Bar." Perhaps nobody has used the tremolo bar on a guitar more and better, creating unbelievable squeals and sounds. Both players could shred leads with the best of them, but Jeff created what is known as the eight-finger technique, tapping at strings with both hands on the neck of the guitar. Nobody had seen that before, and it looked and sounded cool as hell. Tom Morello of Rage Against the Machine and Audioslave is just one of the many current guitar heroes who has told me that he spent days trying to learn how

ABOVE: Jeff Watson and Brad Gillis
OPPOSITE: Kelly Keagy

EDDIE'S PLAYLIST
NIGHT RANGER

1. (YOU CAN STILL) ROCK IN AMERICA
2. DON'T TELL ME YOU LOVE ME
3. DON'T START THINKING
4. TOUCH OF MADNESS
5. SING ME AWAY
6. EDDIE'S COMIN' OUT TONIGHT
7. GROWIN' UP IN CALIFORNIA
8. RUMOURS IN THE AIR
9. TELL YOUR VISION
10. SEVEN WISHES

to do it when he first saw it as a kid. To me, that dual guitar interplay between Brad and Jeff, along with great hook-laden hard rock songs and soaring vocals from two lead singers, is what made Night Ranger special and set them apart from the rest.

Dawn Patrol was followed the next year by *Midnight Madness*, featuring another huge rocker, "(You Can Still) Rock in America." But it is perhaps best known for a ballad written by Keagy about his sister, called "Sister Christian" (her name was Christie). That song became a massive crossover hit for Night Ranger, attracting a whole new audience. The "Sister Christian" video was all over MTV, and suddenly they were being played on multiple radio formats. Hit ballads can often be a double-edged sword for hard rock bands, changing their credibility with hard rock fans, and "Sister Christian" somewhat did that for Night Ranger. That sort of success also does something else: It makes your record label want more of it, and the pressure for the band to produce poppier fare was substantial. To some degree, the band caved in. They had more hits, but their power ballad and move in a more pop direction—and their clean-cut image at a time when the hard rock look dominated—caused their fan base to drift.

Sales began to decline for their fourth album, 1987's *Big Life*, and by the end of the decade, Night Ranger seemed to be finished—at least the classic band looked pretty much done, although several different lineups of Night Ranger existed in coming years. Jack Blades left to form Damn

ABOVE: Jack Blades
OPPOSITE LEFT: Brad Gillis, Eddie, Jack Blades, and Kelly Keagy
OPPOSITE RIGHT: Brad Gillis and Jack Blades

Yankees with Tommy Shaw of Styx, Ted Nugent, and Michael Cartellone (who would later join Lynyrd Skynyrd). That band ran its course after just two albums, and Jack returned to Night Ranger in 1996, giving the band its frontman back and a new life to the classic lineup. Even though some good albums were made during this period, most of them went largely unrecognized. As has been well documented, the mid-'90s were not kind to the MTV hard rock bands of the '80s, to put it mildly. But Night Ranger always made their name as a live act, and continued to tour. In 2007, they created what I thought was their best new studio album in years, *Hole in the Sun*. It was a return to the harder guitar-based rock that made me first love them.

Over the decades, I've become friends with all the guys in the band, and they've done my radio and TV shows countless times. They are so much fun to hang out with, with no rock star B.S.—just good guys who appreciate the music and fans. Jack sent me the song "Tell Your Vision" in advance of *Hole in the Sun*'s release, and it just floored me. To my ears, it was the most rocking thing they had done in a long time. I was really excited about the future of Night Ranger again.

Sadly, with the release of *Hole in the Sun* it was announced that Jeff Watson—a huge part of that twin-guitar assault—was out of the band. I was bummed to hear the news and could never quite figure out why this happened, beyond the usual fallout within bands. Night Ranger replaced him first with Winger guitarist Reb Beach, then current player Joel Hoekstra, who does a phenomenal job. (Joel also performs with the Trans-Siberian Orchestra as well as the Broadway production of *Rock of Ages*.) In 2011, the band released the solid hard rocker *Somewhere in California*, which was a return to their classic sound of big hooks and harmonies. With two solid hard rock albums and a live show as strong as it's ever been, Night Ranger is touring with a wide range of rock acts almost year-round. But it always makes me chuckle when you mention Night Ranger to a hard rock fan. Those who don't know the history simply think of "Sister Christian" and laugh them off as a pop band. Do yourself a favor and go see them live. They still bring it in a big way, and Brad might even play a little Ozzy for you.

TED NUGENT

For nearly five decades, Ted Nugent has been a force in the world of hard rock. The "Motor City Madman" just doesn't care what people think of him, his music, or his beliefs, and I might just love him more for that than for anything else. Now, don't get me wrong. I don't necessarily agree with everything Ted says, but I believe in his right to say it, and man, does Ted exercise his freedom of speech! Because he is such a polarizing figure, I think it's often forgotten that he has made some great music and is a fantastic guitarist. Songs like "Cat Scratch Fever," "Stranglehold," "Great White Buffalo," and "Wango Tango" were the soundtrack of the '70s for many.

CLASSIC LINEUP:

CLIFF DAVIES (DRUMS)

ROB GRANGE (BASS)

TED NUGENT (GUITAR/VOCALS)

DEREK ST. HOLMES (GUITAR/VOCALS)

KEY ADDITIONAL MEMBERS:

BOBBY CHOUINARD (DRUMS)

BRIAN HOWE (VOCALS)

DOUG LUBAHN (BASS)

ALAN ST. JON (KEYBOARDS)

OPPOSITE: Ted Nugent

DISCOGRAPHY

The Amboy Dukes were where it all started for Ted, who became that band's star and lead guitarist at the age of sixteen. Like Nugent himself, the band had roots in Detroit in the mid-'60s, and early on they built a strong following with their psychedelic and at times progressive sound. The band scored mostly regional hits with songs like "Baby Please Don't Go," "Great White Buffalo," and "Journey to the Center of the Mind," many of which Nugent still performs live today. It was clear that Nugent, with his playing and showmanship, was the breakout star of the Amboy Dukes. In fact, they were signed to Frank Zappa's record label and rebranded as Ted Nugent and the Amboy Dukes to capitalize on their rising star.

The group eventually disbanded, but Nugent was such a strong creative force and personality that going solo was an inevitability. In 1975 he released his self-titled debut with a backing band consisting of guitarist/vocalist Derek St. Holmes, drummer Cliff Davies, and bassist Rob Grange. This lineup, widely considered to be the classic Nugent backing band, went on to record the all-time classics *Free-for-All*, *Cat Scratch Fever*, and the live set *Double Live Gonzo!* These albums helped make Nugent a massive star during much of the '70s and a major arena and festival attraction.

Nugent made a name on the live stage not only for his catalog of songs and blazing guitar playing on his signature Gibson Byrdland but also for his over-the-top stage persona and performances. (Ted was notorious for taking the stage in a loincloth like Tarzan!) Ted owned the stage, prowling around like he was possessed, talking to the crowd at a rapid-fire pace, and saying whatever was on his mind—earning him the well-deserved "Motor City Madman" nickname. His blues-influenced guitar licks were infused with a rowdy metal delivery and distortion. As important as his playing was the aggression, power, and volume of it. Nowhere is this bet-

RIGHT: Ted Nugent
OPPOSITE: Derek St. Holmes

er displayed than on *Double Live Gonzo!*, which features one of my all-time favorite crowd raps: when Ted declares, "If anyone here wants to get mellow, they can turn around and get the fuck out of here!" The '70s were the defining era for the double live album, and *Gonzo* is one of the best. Ted's songs took on all-new energy onstage, often expanding into jams that further showcased his ability as a player and his backing band, who were, by that point, truly firing on all cylinders.

Following the monster success of solo albums and tours, the classic Nugent group slowly disbanded, leaving Ted to face the '80s. Artists who had made their names in the '70s often found it hard to maintain their success in the '80s, especially given the birth of music videos. Not only did they have to battle the perception of being yesterday's news, but suddenly image played a huge part as well: It wasn't just what you sounded like but also what you looked like. Nugent actually had a decent run in the '80s, thanks in part to a more commercial sound and a revolving cast of players backing him from album to album, like Carmine Appice, Dave Amato (currently in REO Speedwagon), and Derek St. Holmes from the old days. Of particular note is 1984's *Penetrator*, which saw Ted essentially using Billy Squier's backing band of drummer Bobby Chouinard, bassist Doug Lubahn, and keyboard player Alan St. Jon, joined by British vocalist Brian Howe. This slightly more pop metal approach helped yield Ted a new fan base and ease his transition into the music video world. Songs like *Penetrator*'s "Tied Up in Love" and the title track to 1986's *Little Miss Dangerous* found their way into MTV rotation and connected nicely to the more melodic hard rock of the era. (In fact, a few years after the release of *Penetrator*, English rock band Bad Company enlisted Brian Howe for what was then considered to be the impossible job of replacing their lead singer, Paul Rodgers, and ended up with some huge hit records with Howe fronting the band!)

As much as Ted made strides in the '80s to recapture his glory years, attendance at his concerts was up and down, and he found himself opening for bands like Kiss and Aerosmith—bands he had shared equal status with a decade earlier. It was time for something new, and that meant joining a band for the first time since the Amboy Dukes.

That band was Damn Yankees, the 1990 supergroup with Tommy Shaw of Styx, Jack Blades of Night Ranger, and current Lynyrd Skynyrd drummer Michael Cartellone. Bolstered by the writing talents and vocal abilities of Shaw and Blades, Ted could settle into being just the guitar player. Damn Yankees came roaring out of the gate with a blend of melodic hard rock that was a far cry from the raw, rude approach of Ted's solo work but still featured his stellar, signature guitar wail. The band has made two albums to date and scored major hits with the songs "High Enough" and "Coming of Age." Damn Yankees proved that Ted could work in a band again—and in one that leaned more commercial than what he was known for. But he still had that Ted attitude! Look no further than the video for "High Enough" in which Ted delivers his solo by kicking down a door and emerging in an zebra-striped, ankle-length jacket! The fact that Damn

EDDIE'S PLAYLIST
TED NUGENT

1. JUST WHAT THE DOCTOR ORDERED
2. FREE-FOR-ALL
3. WANG DANG SWEET POONTANG
4. STRANGLEHOLD
5. SNAKESKIN COWBOYS
6. TIED UP IN LOVE
7. LITTLE MISS DANGEROUS
8. STORMTROOPIN'
9. GREAT WHITE BUFFALO
10. HEY BABY

Yankees had such a short run is a mystery to many, including the band members themselves. Their second album, *Don't Tread*, was a bit of a drop-off from their debut, and it didn't take long for everyone to return to the safe haven of their main groups.

These days Ted very much marches to his own beat. Although the door seems to be always open for a Damn Yankees reunion (Ted opened shows for Styx in 2012), Ted, who is now in his sixties, has bigger fish to fry. Or more accurately, animals to hunt! Ted is a well-known and very vocal hunting enthusiast, and his passion for it plays a huge role in what he does and does not do, and if and when he will do it. In 2006 VH1 launched a reality show called *Supergroup* that saw Ted attempting to form a band with Scott Ian, Evan Seinfeld, Jason Bonham, and Sebastian Bach. At the time, I was working as a host for VH1 Classic and was assigned the job of hosting the *Supergroup* postshow. It was a wrap-up program that had me discussing that night's episode with the show's cast. If you saw those postshows, you know there was one member who never appeared: Ted Nugent. And it was for only one reason: When we shot them, it was during hunting season, and nothing stands between Ted and his hunting! Sadly, aside from one live performance, the band formed in that show never saw the light of day.

Today, Ted continues to host and appear on TV, but mostly on shows about hunting and living off the land. His focus seems centered more on his political beliefs, his anti-drug stance, and being an advocate for the right to bear arms than on his music. He still makes a new album every couple of years and tours when it works around his hunting schedule, finding a balance between his passion for music and his love of being the ultimate outdoorsman.

Unfortunately, I've had very few direct personal dealings with Ted in my years in the music industry. The one radio interview I conducted with him was unique in the sense that it was the only one I ever arranged with a publicist that had a *minimum* time requirement! Most artists' reps will say, "Keep it to ten minutes." For Ted it was, "He wants a minimum of thirty minutes or no interview." As a guy who loves to chat, I can respect that, especially since Ted is a well-known talker! In 2012 Ted's mouth actually earned him a visit from the Secret Service when he made public comments that were perceived to be threatening to President Barack Obama. Ted has always been a bit of a magnet for controversy, but I've intentionally kept the focus here on his work as a musician. I think that to many people who are not as well versed in the rock world, his ability as a guitarist is tragically overlooked. It's unfortunate that he's often more known for being a gun-toting conservative loudmouth than for being a phenomenal live performer who made some incredible, classic hard rock music.

LEFT: Ted Nugent

OVERKILL

I've followed Overkill from the beginning, working with these fellow Jersey natives during my days at Megaforce Records and becoming lifelong friends with them. More than twenty-five years after their debut full-length, *Feel the Fire*, Overkill remains, in my opinion, one of the most underrated metal bands in the history of thrash. You hear about the Big Four of thrash—Metallica, Slayer, Anthrax, and Megadeth—but in my personal Big Five, Overkill gets a spot.

CLASSIC LINEUP:

BOBBY "BLITZ" ELLSWORTH (VOCALS)

BOBBY GUSTAFSON (GUITAR)

RAT SKATES (DRUMS)

D.D. VERNI (BASS)

KEY ADDITIONAL MEMBERS:

ROB CANNAVINO (GUITAR)

SID FALCK (DRUMS)

MERRITT GANT (GUITAR)

DAVE LINSK (GUITAR)

RON LIPNICKI (DRUMS)

DEREK TAILER (GUITAR)

OPPOSITE: Bobby Gustafson, Rat Skates, Bobby "Blitz" Ellsworth, and D.D. Verni

DISCOGRAPHY

I saw Overkill in their earliest days, when they played venues like the Showplace in Dover, New Jersey, with the lineup of Rat Skates on drums, Bobby "Blitz" Ellsworth on vocals, D.D. Verni on bass, and Bobby Gustafson on guitar—Gustafson replaced onetime member Dan Spitz, who had joined Anthrax. At that time, the group was more theatrical, with a gothic stage show in which Blitz dressed like a vampire and rose from a cemetery set. They played both covers and originals, on which they meshed the power of heavy metal with the attitude and raw aggression of punk to create their own musical style. Early in Overkill's career, their tracks made their way on the popular tape trading circuit of the day (primitive file sharing!). This helped them land on several popular compilations, such as the *Metal Massacre* series from Metal Blade Records founder Brian Slagel and *New York Metal*. The buzz grew for Overkill, especially on the East Coast, leading to their first proper release, a self-titled four-track EP in 1984.

I was from the same area of New Jersey as Rat Skates and D.D. Verni, and since I was doing one of the only metal shows on commercial radio at the time, I was quickly targeted by the band to help them gain exposure through radio play. On more than one occasion, my mom actually found Overkill demo tapes left in the mailbox for me! Since I truly liked the band and admired their tenacity, I started to play their songs and had them on the show for some interviews—this was a big step for a band that had worked extremely hard to get noticed and was graduating to the big leagues. They earned the attention of Megaforce Records founder Johnny Z, who signed them in 1985 and released their full-length debut, *Feel the Fire*. Reviews were mostly positive, and Overkill took to the road, including a European tour with labelmates Anthrax, which helped them to build the strong following across the pond that still exists to this day.

Overkill's sound really came together with the release of 1987's *Taking Over*—one of the first albums I worked on while at Megaforce and one of my favorite thrash albums of all time. Loud, raw, reckless, and rude, Overkill had strengthened their songwriting to produce future classics like "Powersurge," "Wrecking Crew," and "In Union We Stand," the latter of which also had a brief but nice run on MTV. *Taking Over* was faster and heavier than the band's previous album and uncompromising from start to finish in its speed and riffing. Equally important, *Taking Over* was the first album to benefit from Megaforce's new partnership with Atlantic Records, thus getting major-label support. The band continued touring around the world, both as a headliner doing multiple nights at legendary Brooklyn rock club L'Amour and in support slots for Megadeth and other bands of the early thrash scene.

That same year, Overkill saw their first of many lineup changes, when drummer Rat Skates surprisingly left the group. After working so hard to get the band to this point, Rat departed just when things were really beginning to look up. He started a family, left the music industry, and today still lives in New Jersey and works as a film editor and producer. Overkill was a hardworking and -touring band, and the pace was not for everyone. I recall being at Rat's last show, in Brooklyn, where a big cake was waiting

DID YOU KNOW ?

Bobby Blitz and his wife, Annette, own a gourmet chocolate shop in Nyack, New York, called Chocolaterie. If you go there around Easter, don't be surprised if it's Blitz in the bunny costume out front.

LEFT: Bobby "Blitz" Ellsworth

backstage. He was leaving on good terms, but there was also some sadness and uncertainty with the others that one of the group's most loved members was calling it quits at a crucial time.

Skates was replaced by Sid Falck on 1988's *Under the Influence*, which many feel was a bit of a step back for Overkill—the songs aren't as strong, the mix is off at times, and some of the riffs sound redundant. However, I have always loved it, and the video for "Hello from the Gutter" was a mainstay on MTV and the heavy metal show *Headbangers Ball* back in the day. The band bounced back from the negative critical response to *Under the Influence* with what is widely regarded as their definitive work: 1989's *The Years of Decay*. Produced by Terry Date, best known for his later work with Pantera, the album includes the single and video "Elimination," which became a hit. *The Years of Decay* was a huge leap forward for Overkill in terms of songs, playing, and production, so it came as a surprise in 1990 when it was announced that Bobby Gustafson was leaving the band. Bobby is a sweetheart of a guy, but back in those days, we were all kids, and Bobby drank a bit too much at some shows and rubbed people the wrong way. One of those people was bassist D.D. Verni, who often butted heads with Bobby. Essentially, Gustafson gave Blitz an ultimatum: Either he or Verni had to go. Blitz sided with Verni, Gustafson left, and the rest is Overkill history. Gustafson now lives in Florida and, for the most part, has been inactive in the music business. After Overkill, he played in the female heavy metal band Cycle Sluts from Hell for a brief time, but since leaving them, he has only played with some smaller Florida-based bands.

Gustafson's departure was a pivotal point in the band's career—they

EDDIE'S PLAYLIST

OVERKILL

1. ELECTRIC RATTLESNAKE
2. E.VIL N.EVER D.IES
3. GASOLINE DREAM
4. POWERSURGE
5. OLD SCHOOL
6. ROTTEN TO THE CORE
7. ELECTRO-VIOLENCE
8. HORRORSCOPE
9. ELIMINATION
10. COMA

had made tremendous strides, but now an original member and key component was gone. It also shifted the balance of power in the band, and from that day forward, Overkill has been about two members: Bobby "Blitz" Ellsworth and D.D. Verni. That is not to disparage the many talented musicians who have come and gone in the group; however, it's a simple fact that since this period, all of Overkill's songs have been written by Blitz and D.D., the band is managed by Blitz and D.D., and the albums are created and produced in a studio owned by D.D. Under their guidance, Overkill has pretty much released an album every year or so.

Today, the lineup includes Dave Linsk and Derek Tailer on guitar and more recent addition Ron Lipnicki on drums. Linsk is now the longest-running member outside of Blitz and D.D., and this consistency and quality of musicianship has helped the band make some of their best music in their later years. In 2002 Blitz suffered a stroke in the middle of playing a set with Overkill in Germany. He eventually made a full recovery and often joked with me on my radio show about how crazy it would have been if he had died right onstage, mid-set, with his band. Thankfully, Blitz continues to do what he does best.

In 2005 Overkill invited me to the studio where they were recording their album *Relix IV*. They were cutting a song called "Old School," about the history and the evolution of the band. I was happy to hear that it

ABOVE: Bobby "Blitz" Ellsworth and Eddie
OPPOSITE TOP (clockwise): Bobby Gustafson, Sid Falck, D.D. Verni, and Bobby "Blitz" Ellsworth
OPPOSITE BOTTOM: D.D. Verni, Eddie, Bobby "Blitz" Ellsworth, and Greg D'Angelo of White Lion

featured a line about the first time they were played on the radio, by me! "Who the fuck woulda thunk they're playing us on Eddie Trunk." Bobby Blitz is a true poet! The band also had me record a bit for that same track, as if I were intro'ing them on the radio. Needless to say, it was an amazing honor to be a part of this band's history. "Old School" has actually become a very popular sing-along for the band at shows, and anytime they play it and I'm in attendance, I join them onstage for my part.

Overkill is still a bruising live act, and to me, Blitz is one of the best frontmen in the history of thrash—something Phil Anselmo fought me on during a recent *That Metal Show* episode. (Phil thought *he* was the best, but I've never viewed Pantera as thrash.) Blitz has a way of stalking the stage that conveys the music perfectly. He also has a unique sense of humor and an amazing ability to engage the audience. Why the band hasn't achieved more of an elite status in metal is something I have never been able to figure out. They remain much more popular on the East Coast than on the West, and although they certainly still draw well on the club and theater level, they have never quite crossed over into mainstream popularity. This could be due to the many lineup changes, but it could also be that other than a slot on Dave Mustaine's Gigantour tour in 2006, Overkill was never really taken under a more well-known band's wing and exposed to a larger audience in America. Even though their fan base is loyal, it's hard for the band to bridge beyond it while playing only midsize clubs. As solid as the music is, the sales have stayed largely the same. But this has never bothered Overkill. They found a formula that works for them on their own terms, and as long as they can make a good living doing what they love, it's enough.

As a lifelong fan of the band, and as a friend of both the original and the current members, it's been frustrating to see them sometimes viewed as an afterthought by bigger metal bands, when in reality, they have been at it for just as long and, in my view, have made albums of equal stature.

For this reason, I was truly happy to see Lamb of God singer Randy Blythe turn up on a track called "Skull and Bones" on the band's 2007 release, *Immortalis*. Finally, the influence and consistency of Overkill and what they have created in the metal community was starting to manifest in a new generation of metal bands. In 2012 Overkill released the studio album *The Electric Age*, a metal masterpiece that sounds as fresh and vibrant as *Taking Over* did decades ago. Lipnicki's drumming is simply incredible throughout, and it's perhaps the most old-school thrash album they have made since their early years.

LEFT: Bobby "Blitz" Ellsworth
OPPOSITE TOP LEFT: Dave Linsk
OPPOSITE TOP RIGHT: Bobby Gustafson, Rat Skates, D.D. Verni, and Bobby "Blitz" Ellsworth
OPPOSITE BOTTOM: D.D. Verni

QUEENSRŸCHE

One day in 1983, as a young kid working in a record store, I was busy opening the boxes of new albums that arrived each day. This was always a lot of fun because I'd never know what new release would be arriving from the warehouse and the albums often reached us long before they hit the shelves. As I sifted through a box, a rather plain-looking album with a simple Gothic logo appeared. Nobody in the store had a clue how to pronounce this band's name, but the logo and band certainly looked metal! Complicating matters further was the use of an umlaut in the spelling. When early fans of the group came in to ask for this EP, we laughed at the various pronunciations they came up with. Queens Rich? Queens Rysh? One of my favorites was Queen Cycle—to this day I'm not sure how the dude came up with that pronunciation. But it wasn't long before everyone knew who Queensrÿche was and how to say the band's

CLASSIC LINEUP:

CHRIS DEGARMO (GUITAR)

EDDIE JACKSON (BASS)

SCOTT ROCKENFIELD (DRUMS)

GEOFF TATE (VOCALS)

MICHAEL WILTON (GUITAR)

KEY ADDITIONAL MEMBERS:

KELLY GRAY (GUITAR)

TODD LA TORRE (VOCALS)

PARKER LUNDGREN (GUITAR)

DISCOGRAPHY

BOVE: Eddie and Geoff Tate
GHT: Scott Rockenfield, Michael Wilton, eoff Tate, Eddie Jackson, and Chris eGarmo

Queensrÿche was made up of five young guys who hailed from Bellevue, Washington, and had metal bursting from their veins. The label EMI decided to put out their four-song EP *Queensrÿche* in 1983 as an introduction to the band while they finished working on their debut full-length album. The most stunning thing about the band on first listen was singer Geoff Tate. He could sing in a powerful operatic wail, like an almost-heavy metal Freddie Mercury, and scream with the likes of Rob Halford and Bruce Dickinson. The songs "Queen of the Reich" (the song from which the band derived their name) and "The Lady Wore Black" were immediately hailed as modern metal classics with an epic sound reminiscent of Britain's new wave of heavy metal. The self-titled EP sold on a steady basis, mainly through word of mouth along with some early MTV support. And almost instantly, this new band of youngsters from a Seattle suburb was being put in the same sentence with the big-gun groups that had a huge breakthrough in 1983: Def Leppard, Metallica, Quiet Riot, Iron Maiden, and Judas Priest.

Queensrÿche's full-length debut, *The Warning*, came out the next year, and while it showed the band's growth, introducing some keyboards and other progressive elements, it was still very much full-on metal. The world had taken interest in Queensrÿche, and the video for "Take Hold of the Flame" showed clips of the band's recent visit to Japan, where they were wildly embraced. I saw Queensrÿche many times in these early days, both playing clubs as a headliner and opening for Kiss. They were a hungry, powerful band that gave Kiss a run for their money with their aggressive songs and precise playing. The dual guitars of Chris DeGarmo and Michael Wilton played perfectly off each other, and the rhythm section of bassist Eddie Jackson and drummer Scott Rockenfield was a beast to watch and listen to. But everyone was talking about Tate, and his incredible range and power, both on the album and live onstage.

What stands out about Queensrÿche is their musical evolution. From the very beginning, there was no doubt the band was pure metal, but by their third release, 1986's *Rage for Order*, it had become clear that they weren't going to stay stuck in the denim-and-leather metal world. *Rage for Order* saw a huge leap in the band's look and sound. Visually, they adopted an almost futuristic glam look (not in a Poison-wearing-lipstick sense, but more like '80s new wave meets sci-fi). And musically, they brought in synthesizers in a more prominent way and textured progressive elements. The song "Gonna Get Close to You" is just downright weird for its time, though its video—which conveys both the creepy atmosphere and the unusual progression of the song—got some traction on MTV. For the small number of metal purists who may have jumped the Queensrÿche ship at this time, just as many new fans came on board and found it interesting to see a band constantly push into new areas while still being true to metal.

This all set up what many feel is the band's defining moment, the 1988 concept album *Operation: Mindcrime*. At the height of the MTV era, not many hard rock bands were composing full-blown concept albums at such a pivotal point in their career, but Queensrÿche was. The album's story line is about a junkie turned hit man who works for an underground political movement. What could have been a bomb became the band's strongest hook. *Mindcrime* was a critical and commercial hit, with the songs "I Don't Believe in Love," "Speak," and the title track all getting major airplay. The band graduated to arenas, where they played the album in its entirety with an extensive stage show. *Mindcrime* was even being mentioned in the same breath as other concept masterpieces, like *The Wall* by Pink Floyd and *2112* by Rush. For their follow-up, 1990's *Empire*, Queensrÿche again showed their interest in taking risks by using orchestral arrangements on the power ballad "Silent Lucidity," which was a huge crossover smash. Few bands have grown as writers and performers as quickly as Queensrÿche did.

But *Empire* proved to be the end of what many consider the definitive era of Queensrÿche. Almost nonstop touring had taken its toll on the band, and there was a four-year break before *Promised Land* was released. Reaction was mixed, as it was again in 1997 when *Hear in the Now Frontier* came out. A major blow to the group took place at this time in the form of its first lineup change. *Hear in the Now Frontier* was the final album for guitarist Chris DeGarmo, who decided to leave the touring life following its release. This was bigger than Queensrÿche just losing a guitar player. Chris was a major creative force in the writing department, and his departure left a huge void that some feel the band has never recovered from. Although DeGarmo has since contributed by writing songs with the band, for all intents and purposes, he is out of the music industry and now a pilot for an industrial aviation firm. Queensrÿche fans constantly ask about Chris coming back to the band (which no doubt has irked the remaining band members in the years he has been gone).

Queensrÿche moved forward with several different replacements in the second guitar slot, most recently Parker Lundgren, who, for a brief time, was Geoff Tate's son-in-law. The band has released several albums since, including a sequel to *Operation: Mindcrime* (which features the

EDDIE'S PLAYLIST

QUEENSRŸCHE

1. THE LADY WORE BLACK
2. QUEEN OF THE REICH
3. WALK IN THE SHADOWS
4. IF I WERE KING
5. WARNING
6. TAKE HOLD OF THE FLAME
7. I DON'T BELIEVE IN LOVE
8. EYES OF A STRANGER
9. BEST I CAN
10. EMPIRE

great Ronnie James Dio) and another concept album, called *American Soldier*. Reaction to the band's later music has been mixed. The hard-core fans love every progressive move and experimentation, while the rockers scream for a return to traditional metal.

I have known the guys in the band almost since day one and have recorded countless radio and TV interviews with them. They're all good guys and I like them very much, but I could tell that a tension was brewing in the band, and it really started to peak with several strange moves. First, the band performed an "adults only" rock show called "The Queensrÿche Cabaret." This was seen as pushing the envelope a bit too far and was snickered at by many. Queensrÿche as a cabaret act, complete with scantily clad dancers (and a scantily clad Geoff Tate)? Then, in 2011, the band released *Dedicated to Chaos*, which was their least metal album yet. In interviews, Geoff staunchly defended these questionable decisions, saying it's always important to try new things. In fairness to him, Queensrÿche always has been about evolution, but many felt this went too far. The band had become a Tate vehicle in the minds of many fans, not just because he was its leader and singer but also because his wife worked as its manager, his daughter worked with the merchandise, and his son-in-law was given a gig as guitarist. This all led to an epic blowup in April 2012, with tensions in the band reaching such a level that it actually got physical. Words were

ABOVE: Geoff Tate

exchanged backstage at a show in Brazil, punches were thrown, and Geoff later admitted on *That Metal Show* that he did indeed spit on drummer Scott Rockenfield during the performance. Everyone had to be separated after the show, and the band went one way and the Tates went the other.

Shortly after this incident, I hosted two of the band's final shows: one in Maryland at the M3 Rock Festival and one in Oklahoma at Rocklahoma. Rumors of the blowup were everywhere and those in the know were shocked that the band didn't cancel the shows. At these last gigs, Geoff and the rest of the band were kept separate, only together for the hour or so onstage, but you could still see the tension. For example, at Rocklahoma, I was providing live TV coverage for HDNet and Tate would only talk with me before the show, and Wilton and Rockenfield after. It's always strange when stuff like this happens with bands you know and love. I try not to take sides and instead give both parties a fair platform to air their version of things. Shortly after the Oklahoma gig, the band went public with their feud and all hell broke loose.

After continued fighting, Geoff Tate released a solo metal album and also launched a new version of Queensrÿche. The rest of the band also came forward with their new lineup of Queensrÿche with a Tate sound-alike by the name of Todd La Torre, from the group Crimson Glory. In August 2012, I welcomed Geoff as a guest on *That Metal Show* and he told his side of the story, saying that all the members of Queensrÿche had an equal vote in everything the band did. He didn't feel it was fair to paint him as the villain who made all the creative and business decisions. He seemed genuinely stung by the crazy course of events surrounding Queensrÿche, and by the fact that he was essentially kicked out of his own band. In February 2013, I had Scott Rockenfield on my radio show to share his viewpoint and to premiere the first song without Tate, called "Redemption." It was a return to their classic, heavy sound. Unfortunately, at this time, it's still unclear what the future holds for the band, and which side will ultimately win ownership of the name Queensrÿche.

LEFT: Parker Lundgren, Eddie Jackson, and Michael Wilton
ABOVE: Todd La Torre

QUIET RIOT

uiet Riot is best known as the band that scored the huge hits "Cum on Feel the Noize" and "Metal Health" back in 1983 with their U.S. debut album, *Metal Health*. But maybe even more important, they're the band that introduced the world to the late, great guitarist Randy Rhoads. Pre-*Metal Health*, most metal fans in America—outside of clubgoers on the West Coast in the '70s—were unaware of Randy and Quiet Riot. But the truth is that Quiet Riot launched in the L.A. area as early as 1973 and often gigged with bands like Van Halen and other upstarts of the Southern California rock scene. Quiet Riot's original lineup consisted of Rhoads, vocalist Kevin DuBrow, bassist Kelly Garni, and drummer Drew Forsyth, and they made quite a name for themselves on the club circuit with their killer mix of anthemic hard rock, a flamboyant frontman in DuBrow, and the amazing playing of Rhoads, who meshed his classical influences with a full-on metal assault. Randy's style was rawer in the Quiet Riot days, but they proved to be important years in shaping one of rock's most legendary players.

CLASSIC LINEUP:

FRANKIE BANALI (DRUMS)

CARLOS CAVAZO (GUITAR)

KEVIN DUBROW (VOCALS)

RUDY SARZO (BASS)

KEY ADDITIONAL MEMBERS:

DREW FORSYTH (DRUMS)

KELLY GARNI (BASS)

SEAN MCNABB (BASS)

RANDY RHOADS (GUITAR)

PAUL SHORTINO (VOCALS)

CHUCK WRIGHT (BASS)

DISCOGRAPHY

It seemed like a combination that couldn't fail, but for whatever reason, the band wasn't able to secure a U.S. record deal. They were signed to CBS Records in 1977, but strangely enough, only in Japan, where *Quiet Riot* and *Quiet Riot II* were released in the late '70s—and to this day are available in America only as imports. These albums became especially significant after Randy Rhoads was tragically killed in a plane crash in March of '82. By then, he had left Quiet Riot and was a member of Ozzy Osbourne's band, but after his death, the world searched for any recordings they could find that featured his incredible playing.

Quiet Riot is notorious for its many lineup changes over the years. It was actually a relaunched version of the band in 1983 that provided the group with its huge success and increased profile stateside. The new lineup of DuBrow, guitarist Carlos Cavazo, bassist Rudy Sarzo (who, along with Rhoads, had played with Ozzy Osbourne), and drummer Frankie Banali was finally signed to a U.S. label called Pasha, a subsidiary of CBS and the imprint of producer Spencer Proffer, who produced the band's first U.S. release, the smash hit *Metal Health*. Quiet Riot's U.S. debut was a very important album in the history of heavy metal, both because it sold millions of copies and because it was the first metal album to reach number one on the *Billboard* charts and to have a song to hit the Top 5. The band proved that their style of music could not only sell tons of copies but also get radio and video exposure in the new era of MTV.

Metal Health was an album I could point to while working in a record store and say to people, "Look, metal sells! People want to hear it!" I can't tell you how many LPs and cassettes of *Metal Health* I rang up, and it felt great to see a band that I loved and supported ringing the register. The popularity of Quiet Riot, along with Metallica, Def Leppard, and Iron Maiden, helped me get my first-ever metal radio show on the air.

It's hard to believe now, but back in 1983 these bands were struggling to break, and radio didn't really know what to do with them. The huge pop and new wave bands of the '70s were dominating. Sure, there were the older metal bands at the time, but they didn't get much airplay either. An accessible metal band was what rock fans needed to turn the tide. And here came Quiet Riot, a catchy band with big hooks and choruses, but also one with a tough look and DuBrow's howling screams. This was the start of a new era of American West Coast metal, and bands like Ratt, Mötley Crüe, and W.A.S.P. rode Quiet Riot's wave.

Thanks to the success of the album's title track and a cover of the Slade song "Cum on Feel the Noize," Quiet Riot became a household name and had credibility seemingly overnight, even though DuBrow had already been fighting to make it for ten years! At the time, I was a nineteen-year-old kid doing one of the first metal radio shows in the country, and DuBrow was one of my earliest interviews. I don't remember all that much about the experience, but being so new to the game, it felt great getting in on the ground floor of a band's rise to the top, although it was clear that DuBrow already had so much history. His experience had given him confidence, and he knew how to handle the press.

One would think that the massive success of *Metal Health* would set the stage for a lengthy career, but it only set up one of the most shocking and rapid crashes rock has ever seen. Quiet Riot's follow-up, 1984's *Condition Critical*, sold about half of what their U.S. debut had. There was a backlash from fans who quickly dismissed the band as formulaic. Having yet another Slade cover as their lead single, "Mama Weer All Crazee Now" (DuBrow loved British glam and hard rock, and borrowed from it often), didn't help the perception that maybe there wasn't all that much substance to the band. Factor in that Iron Maiden, Metallica, Judas Priest, and other metal groups were now very popular, and the landscape for Quiet Riot was suddenly very competitive.

It was also around this time that DuBrow's ego seemingly became inflated beyond control. He would often go on crazy tirades, taking shots at other bands, and seemed to hold a general belief that everyone owed him for opening the doors to the metal scene. He once even dared to mention his band in the same breath with the Beatles. Soon enough, the press and fans started to turn on Kevin. I personally never had a negative experience with him, but many journalists did. Instead of being a beloved figure of one of rock's biggest bands, Kevin found that the world was quickly beginning to root against him, including his own band members—Rudy Sarzo jumped ship to join Whitesnake. DuBrow was also partying hard, which only added to his unfiltered rants in the press.

Moving forward despite the controversy, the band released *QR III* in 1986, featuring the great single "The Wild and the Young" (a song I personally love because it captures the spirit of the band's past hits with a slightly more modern production), but it was all pretty much over. Radio and MTV, which had previously declared Quiet Riot the darlings of the time, drifted away, and instead many of the new metal bands that Quiet Riot had helped open the door for took their place on playlists. In 1987, Quiet Riot fired DuBrow from his own band and replaced him with

TOP: Kevin DuBrow and Randy Rhoads
BOTTOM: Frankie Banali and Eddie
OPPOSITE RIGHT: Rudy Sarzo, Frankie Banali, Kevin DuBrow, and Carlos Cavazo
OPPOSITE LEFT: Carlos Cavazo

EDDIE'S PLAYLIST
QUIET RIOT

1. MAMA WEER
   ALL CRAZEE NOW
2. FREE
3. THE WILD AND THE YOUNG
4. LOOK IN ANY WINDOW
5. THUNDERBIRD
6. SLICK BLACK CADILLAC
7. LAUGHING GAS
8. METAL HEALTH
9. BREATHLESS
10. TROUBLE

ABOVE: Kevin DuBrow and Randy Rhoads
OPPOSITE: Kevin DuBrow

Paul Shortino. While certainly a risky move, replacing their inflammatory singer was the only chance for the rest of the band to get a fair shake. But it didn't matter. Quiet Riot was already a joke in the metal world, and 1988's *QR*, Shortino's debut on lead, was a bomb. By 1989, less than six years after ruling the arenas, radio, and MTV, Quiet Riot was finished.

A kinder, gentler DuBrow eventually returned to Quiet Riot in the early '90s, but interest in the band wasn't renewed. I hosted several shows for the band at small clubs in Queens—the only gigs they could get—but few people showed up. However, over the years, people came to love Kevin again and chalked up his over-the-top behavior to a sign of the times (and maybe one too many substances). I'll say this for Kevin: He was always very cool to me, and no matter if I was seeing him at Madison Square Garden or a basement club in Queens playing to forty people, he always brought it hard onstage. He fronted the band like a madman, leaving the audience no choice but to get into it. Kevin would force you to clap and sing, and then he would jump into the crowd and have a drink with you, spinning his black-and-white-striped mic stand with reckless abandon. In my opinion, he was a massively underrated live entertainer.

As the mid-2000s rolled around, the band started to get some traction on the festival circuit, and suddenly the anthemic "Metal Health" and "Cum on Feel the Noize" were being played over the PA at sports stadiums everywhere. In August 2007 I hosted the first ever Rocklahoma Festival, in Pryor, Oklahoma, with Quiet Riot in the lineup. I was happy to see the band finally getting some attention and moving beyond the stigma against them. I spent some time talking with Kevin that hot and sweaty afternoon. He seemed really excited that things were finally starting to look up for his music and that there was renewed interest in the band. There have been many stories of his drug use over the decades, but he appeared healthy and sober that day and turned in a great performance. Little did I know that when I introduced the band to the festival rockers, it would be the last time I would see Kevin, and one of the last shows he would ever play. In November 2007, Kevin DuBrow was found dead in his home in Las Vegas from a cocaine overdose. Had it happened a decade or two earlier, this news wouldn't have been a shock. However, by 2007 Kevin had, by all accounts, seemed to have turned a corner. Sadly, his demons would not let go.

The Quiet Riot family tree is long and complex. From their early lineups of the '70s right through to the albums they made till Kevin's passing, many musicians passed through the ranks. These days, drummer Frankie Banali owns the band's name, and following Kevin's death, Frankie claimed the band would die with its undisputed leader. However, after a brief period of mourning, Banali has once again launched a lineup of the band in which he is now the only member from the *Metal Health* period. The new Quiet Riot exists as more of a celebration of the music Kevin made famous than anything else. Quiet Riot made its mark on metal in many ways, but sadly, like their frontman, they crashed and burned too soon.

DID YOU KNOW

Marilyn Manson played a huge role in Quiet Riot getting back together. Around 2001, he reunited the *Metal Health* lineup to perform at an afterparty for a Manson show.

It's hard to overstate how huge Quiet Riot was on the 70's L.A. club scene. Eddie Van Halen even used to go out to see them to scout the competition.

UNDERGROUND CLASSIC

Check out Kevin DuBrow's 2004 solo album, *In for the Kill*. A huge fan of classic British hard rock, he covered songs by Queen, the Sweet, T. Rex, Deep Purple, and others.

RATT

've always found it strange that Ratt, one of the major hard rock bands to come out of the '80s, isn't held in higher regard in the rock world today. In my view, they are right up there with Mötley Crüe, Whitesnake, and the other bands that emerged at the same time and on the same scene. Ratt had a long run of hugely successful albums, many bona fide top radio hits, groundbreaking videos, and music that still holds up remarkably well today.

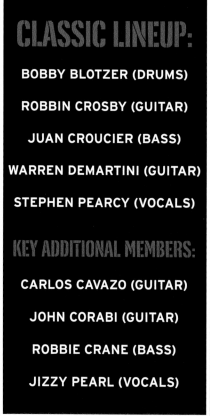

CLASSIC LINEUP:

BOBBY BLOTZER (DRUMS)

ROBBIN CROSBY (GUITAR)

JUAN CROUCIER (BASS)

WARREN DEMARTINI (GUITAR)

STEPHEN PEARCY (VOCALS)

KEY ADDITIONAL MEMBERS:

CARLOS CAVAZO (GUITAR)

JOHN CORABI (GUITAR)

ROBBIE CRANE (BASS)

JIZZY PEARL (VOCALS)

OPPOSITE: Warren DeMartini,
Stephen Pearcy, and Carlos Cavazo

DISCOGRAPHY

ABOVE: Stephen Pearcy
OPPOSITE LEFT: Robbin Crosby
OPPOSITE RIGHT: Warren DeMartini

Ratt dates back to the late '70s in San Diego, where Stephen Pearcy fronted a band called Mickey Ratt, in which future Ozzy Osbourne guitarist Jake E. Lee also played. Around 1983 the band relocated to Los Angeles and shortened their name to Ratt. Drummer Bobby Blotzer and bassist Juan Croucier were recruited from an early version of Dokken, while guitarist Warren DeMartini came on board to replace Lee, who had landed the gig in Ozzy's band. Second guitarist Robbin Crosby also came on to complete what would become the definitive Ratt lineup. The band's sound has always been hook-laden hard rock, and their early recordings certainly had those qualities, although with a very raw edge. Their demo recordings landed them a deal with a small independent label called Time Coast, which released their first EP *Ratt*. Sadly, this EP is tough to find these days and has never properly come out on CD, and due to a typical bad business deal by a then very young band, Ratt still doesn't have control over its release or the rights to the recordings. But the EP set the stage for much bigger things, namely a deal with Atlantic Records and the release of their full-length debut, *Out of the Cellar*, in 1984.

Ratt burst onto the scene in a huge way. Their sound was accessible but also tough, delivered with a snarling attitude. Pearcy had a certain charisma and a unique quality to his voice that more than made up for any shortcomings he had as a singer. In DeMartini, the band had their guitar hero, and though often shy and reserved, he laid down licks and solos that were tasteful and exciting to listen to. Ratt seemed to have it all. They were commercial, but not so commercial that they would alienate the harder rock audience, and their music was enjoyed by women as much as men. *Out of the Cellar*'s lead single, "Round and Round," found a home on radio and TV and, along with other early hits "Back for More" and "Wanted Man," made the band a smash seemingly overnight.

Ratt's videos played a huge role in their success. They were elaborate, expensive productions, often with story lines and actors, and of course with scantily clad women. Many were surprised at Hollywood legend Milton Berle's cameo appearance in more than one of the band's videos, not knowing that Berle's nephew was the band's manager at the time. Another key factor was producer Beau Hill, who did a great job in getting that Ratt sound—the perfect blend of harmony and heavy punch. Hill produced many of the band's biggest albums, and I think he is a big reason why they still sound so good today. (That and, of course, killer songs with great hooks and searing guitars.)

Invasion of Your Privacy followed in 1985 with more hit singles and videos for songs like "Lay It Down" and "You're in Love." In 1986 Ratt released *Dancing Undercover*, featuring the hits "Dance" and one of my all-time favorite Ratt songs, "Body Talk." That year proved to be a big one for the band and saw them graduate to headlining arenas. I even saw Ratt headline Madison Square Garden on their tour in support of *Dancing Undercover*—an incredible feat for a band that had burst onto the scene just a few years earlier. I recall attending an afterparty for this major moment in Ratt history at a Manhattan restaurant called Dish of Salt. It

was a huge celebration, and the vibe in the music industry was that Ratt would be a major band and were on their way to building a legacy like their own heroes Van Halen and Aerosmith. What nobody knew on that night was that trouble was brewing in the world of Ratt, and the future wasn't as bright as everyone thought.

Ratt continued to make really strong albums, like 1988's *Reach for the Sky* and 1990's *Detonator*, scoring more big hits and massively popular videos. Even though the songs started to get a bit more pop metal, polished, and radio friendly, they still contained the band's signature brash "Ratt 'n' Roll" vibe. But around 1990, touring, partying, and the pressure to produce hits started to take a toll on the band. For *Detonator*, they parted ways with Beau Hill and enlisted outside writing help from song doctors Desmond Child and Diane Warren. Jon Bon Jovi makes an appearance on the album as well. Despite the fact that Ratt moved away from their edgier sound, it's important to note that, as a fan, I don't recall anyone thinking Ratt had sold out. It just felt like the natural evolution going on at the time. And while many bands had power ballads that drove their careers, Ratt never relied on them.

UNDERGROUND CLASSIC

Check out the self-titled debut album from Arcade, the group Pearcy formed with Fred Coury of Cinderella after leaving Ratt.

EDDIE'S PLAYLIST

RATT

1. YOU THINK YOU'RE TOUGH
2. YOU'RE IN TROUBLE
3. NEVER USE LOVE
4. WANTED MAN
5. BODY TALK
6. NOBODY RIDES FOR FREE
7. EAT ME UP ALIVE
8. BACK FOR MORE
9. LAY IT DOWN
10. DANCE

TOP: Warren DeMartini and
Stephen Pearcy
BOTTOM: Bobby Blotzer
OPPOSITE: Warren DeMartini,
Carlos Cavazo, Eddie, Robbie Crane,
and Stephen Pearcy

The big problems were what was happening internally within the band. Guitarist Robbin Crosby, a key songwriter, was battling drug addiction. "King," as Crosby, a huge hulking figure, was known, was hooked on heroin, and things reached a breaking point in 1991 while the band was touring Japan. It was the last time Crosby performed with Ratt, who then dismissed him in hopes that he would get help. Crosby was close with Nikki Sixx, who was also battling addiction at the time. And while Nikki came out on the other side and eventually got clean, Robbin was not as fortunate. In 2001 he was diagnosed with HIV, and in 2002 he died of a heroin overdose.

Crosby was replaced for a short time by Michael Schenker, but things were already pretty much over. In the time between Robbin being fired and his passing, the ride got very bumpy for Ratt, not only because of the departure of a key member but also because of the usual egos and infighting. The change in musical tastes didn't help this '80s rock band either, and by 1993 Pearcy formed another band called Arcade, while DeMartini had a short stint in Whitesnake. Ratt was done for the balance of the '90s, until Blotzer and DeMartini put a new version of the band together with Love/Hate singer Jizzy Pearl. Diluting things further was Pearcy's own version of Ratt, which was also making the rounds. Both were playing clubs on most nights, and although both were fun to go see,

neither was truly Ratt. In 2007, I was asked to consult on and host a new rock festival in Oklahoma called Rocklahoma. It was at that first Rocklahoma that Ratt finally reunited with Pearcy. In addition to Blotzer and DeMartini, the lineup included former Mötley Crüe singer John Corabi on guitar and Robbie Crane on bass. It was a solid return to form for the band that had been sharing a bill once again with Poison in 2007, but to me, the vibe never seemed right then or since.

In the past six years, Ratt's levels of musical activity and band dysfunction have been up and down. In 2010 they released a new studio album called *Infestation* with former Quiet Riot guitarist Carlos Cavazo on second guitar. While the album was good, it seems like egos and disagreements continue to cause bumps in the road, preventing this band from fully embracing the position they should have had as one of the dominant forces of '80s hard rock. Pearcy seems content to perform with Ratt or to work on his own projects and solo band. And it was announced that Blotzer was joining a new lineup of Queensrÿche. There just doesn't seem to be the level of total commitment needed from all the key members to make it all work. Ratt made one live appearance in 2012, performing at another festival I host called M3 in Maryland. In an interview to promote it on my radio show, Pearcy announced that bassist Juan Croucier would make a return to the lineup after years of being away. Croucier was a much-missed member of the band, not only as a player but also for his vocals. It was a good show, and I had a blast hanging with the guys that weekend. It seemed like "Ratt 'n' Roll" might finally be back full time, but it ended up being the only show they did that year. Going forward, Ratt plans to make a new album and announced new tour dates in 2013, but it's anyone's guess where that will lead. As a fan, it's frustrating to see a band that was so talented not deliver on a more consistent level, but their classic albums continue to be some of the finest hard rock the

RIOT

Riot, not to be confused with Quiet Riot, was a New York City–based band that came on the scene in the mid-'70s. Of all the bands in this book, they may be the most underappreciated and the unluckiest. But those readers who know of the greatness of their landmark albums are already aware of why they are included here.

Riot was formed by guitarist Mark Reale, singer Guy Speranza, drummer Peter Bitelli, and bassist Phil Feit. The group was clearly influenced by the early British hard rock of Zeppelin, Humble Pie, and others. However, Riot found a way to take those styles and infuse them with more energy and a contemporary vibe, with Speranza's clean, soaring voice and songs with strong hooks that you could grab on to and bang your head. But unfortunately, from the start, Riot seemed to be doomed by bad decisions.

CLASSIC LINEUP:

KIP LEMMING (BASS)

MARK REALE (GUITAR)

SANDY SLAVIN (DRUMS)

GUY SPERANZA (VOCALS)

RICK VENTURA (GUITAR)

KEY ADDITIONAL MEMBERS:

PETER BITELLI (DRUMS)

MIKE DIMEO (VOCALS)

PHIL FEIT (BASS)

RHETT FORRESTER (VOCALS)

JIMMY IOMMI (BASS)

BOBBY JARZOMBEK (DRUMS)

L.A. KOUVARIS (GUITAR)

DON VAN STAVERN (BASS)

OPPOSITE: Guy Speranza

DISCOGRAPHY

The group was very much run by its leader, Reale, but they teamed up with Billy Arnell and Steve Loeb, who became the band's managers, producers, and record label. Yes, you read that right! In the beginning, Arnell and Loeb were all three for Riot—chalk that up as mistake number one. Arnell and Loeb also owned the studio where Riot recorded their debut, *Rock City*, released in 1977 on Loeb and Arnell's Fire Sign Records. I'm not insinuating that Arnell and Loeb didn't have the band's best interests in mind, but most artists would agree that having some separation is good in order to avoid possible conflicts of interest. Management is supposed to push a label to support an album, but that's hard to do when all parties fall under one roof!

Rock City received less-than-stellar reviews but found an audience with the metal faithful. During a time when disco and new wave were dominating the music scene, a heavy rock band from New York with no real fashion sense or image was a long shot for breaking out. *Rock City* was the first in Riot's series of bad album covers—some of the worst in metal history—featuring an evil seal known as the Mighty Tior, which served as a kind of mascot for the band. Album number two, *Narita*, was named after an airport in Japan, because the band had had some early support overseas, but even though it contained more great hard rock, it ended up being released only in Japan at the time.

Soon, the inevitable lineup changes began, with drummer Sandy Slavin coming on board, Rick Ventura joining on second guitar, and Kip Lemming taking over on bass, rounding out what is widely considered to be the band's classic lineup. This is when Riot really came into their own. The band had some of its best players, and the guitar interplay between Ventura and Reale was a real highlight.

The band's third album, *Fire Down Under*, is one of hard rock's all-time

greatest undiscovered gems. It has a live energy, a brilliant assault, that jumps out instantly. The writing is spot-on, with catchy hooks, incredible riffs, and those guitar trade-offs between Reale and Ventura bolstered by the great in-the-pocket rhythm section of Lemming and Slavin. It seemed as if Riot had worked out all the early struggles and growing pains, put together the right lineup, and were finally firing on all cylinders. Don't get me wrong, there are some truly great moments on the first two Riot albums, but *Fire Down Under* is head and shoulders better in all areas (except the cover, which once again featured the Mighty Tior). Steve Loeb, producer of the album, seemed to really have it down in the studio this time around, and with monster tracks like "Swords and Tequila," "Feel the Same," "Outlaw," and "Altar of the King," *Fire Down Under* should have been the album that made them a household name. But it didn't.

Fire Down Under was recorded for Capitol Records, but the label decided not to release it after a dispute with Riot's management over a song called "You're All I Needed Tonight." Capitol wanted the song on the album, but the band's management (i.e., Loeb and Arnell) refused, feeling it was a bit too commercial. The resulting power play crippled the band, by cutting off their cash flow and creating bad blood with their label. After the band's management orchestrated a public campaign to get the album released, the recording was eventually sold to Elektra. But the damage was done and the band was viewed as damaged goods in the music industry. Despite the brilliance of *Fire Down Under*, the ordeal of getting it out into the market cast another black cloud over this great band, and although the metal press and fans loved it, the album failed to produce any level of commercial breakthrough success. It didn't help matters that a band called Quiet Riot was about to explode on the scene and confuse audiences about which band was which.

ABOVE: Mark Reale
LEFT: Rick Ventura and Kip Lemming
OPPOSITE RIGHT: Mark Reale, Sandy Slavin, Rhett Forrester, Kip Lemming, the Mighty Tior, and Rick Ventura
OPPOSITE LEFT: Rhett Forrester

ABOVE: Sandy Slavin
RIGHT: Rhett Forrester and Mark Reale

It can't be denied that *Fire Down Under* lifted Riot to greater heights than they had previously achieved, and they were able to tour America in support of it, opening for the likes of Grand Funk and Rush. But just as things started to look like they would finally explode for this talented band, another huge bombshell hit: Guy Speranza, their talented vocalist, announced he was leaving. Guy had a great voice for hard rock and was a key writer of the band's material—his decision to leave could not have come at a worse time.

I was too young to know the guys in Riot in 1982-83, but in later years I got to know Sandy Slavin very well and had Mark Reale on my radio shows with later versions of the band. By all accounts, Guy was a reserved man who wasn't really up for the constant grind of touring as he grew older. He had already slugged it out for a while by the time Riot started touring for *Fire Down Under* and was interested in pursuing a more regular job and raising a family off the road. Many fans are shocked when they hear about super-talented musicians who opt to check out of the rock world. However, the reality is that the lifestyle simply isn't for everyone, and Guy had had enough. Amazingly, he played a final show opening for Rush in 1981 in New Jersey and then completely left the music business behind to become an exterminator. The frontman for one of hard rock's greatest new bands, which had just made a masterpiece album, left music for pest control!

Riot decided to continue on and soon replaced Speranza with singer Rhett Forrester. Where Guy's voice had a high, clean sound, Rhett's was gravelly, with a swagger and attitude in the style of Bon Scott. It worked well on the two studio albums Riot made with Rhett—*Restless Breed* and *Born in America*—but there wasn't a fan I knew who didn't miss Guy and hope for his return. It was during the live shows, when Rhett sang the old material, that fans most missed Guy; it just wasn't the same without him.

The loss of a key member at a key time, coupled with the lack of success, caused Riot to fold in 1984. After finishing a brief tour supporting Kiss, they called it quits in New York with a final show at L'Amour in Brooklyn, which I attended. The hope was that maybe after a break, Guy would return and the band would be able to pick up where they had left off, but it was not to be.

Riot eventually did reunite, but not with Speranza. In fact, Mark Reale, who was always the band's driving force, went on to release ten more albums with a constantly changing band around him. The band was always trying out different styles—progressive at times, experimental at others, and even using horns on the album *The Privilege of Power*. The band was reaching and was losing its sense of identity. Outside of a brief moment when Riot released an album called *Thundersteel*, which some fans felt was a return to their classic sound, for the most part, the band ended that night in 1984 at L'Amour. (And for many, it was over the day Guy walked away a few years earlier.) For me, it was the strong songwriting and the voice of Speranza that had put this band on the map. You simply can't go wrong with any of the band's first three albums, all of which have been reissued over the years by various labels as new fans discover their greatness. I would even say that *Fire Down Under* is one of the greatest hard rock/metal albums of all time.

If Riot's lack of mainstream success is viewed by their fans as a music-business tragedy, a real-life tragedy is sadly the final chapter in the band's saga. At just forty-seven years old, Guy Speranza passed away from cancer in 2003. He was still working as an exterminator at the time of his death, and his family believes his illness was brought on by his near-constant exposure to chemicals. In recent years, I have heard from members of Guy's family, thanking me for spreading the word to today's metal fans about the great music he made. Sadly, Rhett Forrester also died in 1994, having been shot in the streets of Atlanta after running with the wrong crowd.

In December 2011, Mark Reale assembled a lineup of Riot that celebrated the *Thundersteel* era of the band—the most successful period outside of the early years. They booked a date at B.B. King's Blues Club in New York, and I was happy to come on board to help promote the event. Even though the glory days of Riot were over for me, I thought that it would still be fun to see what Mark had put together and that I'd get to hear a couple of tracks from *Fire Down Under*. I was in the process of arranging an interview with Mark to support the show when it was announced he would not be playing it because of illness. Mark had suffered from Crohn's disease for most of his life, and it had recently flared up, forcing him off the road. A short time later, in January 2012, Mark Reale passed away.

Riot is very much the story of an amazing band that should have been huge but never got the breaks they needed. Bad timing, bad business, bad decisions, bad luck—they all conspired against Riot. But nothing can ever wipe away the greatness of those early albums. Do yourself a favor, and pick up *Fire Down Under* if you want to explore some amazing hard rock. I assure you, you will be blown away.

UNDERGROUND CLASSIC

Recorded in 1981 and originally released only in Japan in 1989, *Riot Live* is one of the few proper live recordings of the band featuring Guy Speranza.

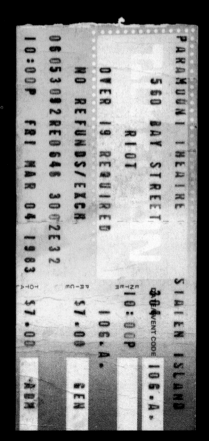

SAXON

As a young kid in high school, I was consumed, as you might expect, by all things hard rock and metal. One of the things I loved most was discovering new bands that my friends hadn't heard of yet and then turning people on to them. This was a couple of years before I started in radio, but in the halls of my school, among the very few metal fans I knew, I was considered the guy who had the scoop on what was the next big thing in the genre. My high school years of 1979 to '82 were a fertile time for metal coming from England. A movement called the New Wave of British Heavy Metal was a huge story in the U.K. and was gaining traction in America. How did we know about NWOBHM (as it's almost always abbreviated)? The British press. This was, of course, long before the Internet and computers in every home, so we relied on the British magazines, and my bible at the time was a magazine called *Kerrang!* I would travel to a record store about twenty minutes from my house called Vintage Vinyl (which still exists in New Jersey!) every other week to buy this import mag and some import albums.

CLASSIC LINEUP:

PETER "BIFF" BYFORD (VOCALS)

STEVE DAWSON (BASS)

NIGEL GLOCKLER (DRUMS)

GRAHAM OLIVER (GUITAR)

PAUL QUINN (GUITAR)

KEY ADDITIONAL MEMBERS:

NIBBS CARTER (BASS)

PETE GILL (DRUMS)

DOUG SCARRATT (GUITAR)

OPPOSITE: Biff Byford and Paul Quinn

DISCOGRAPHY

NWOBHM was, at its core, a reaction against much of the punk music flooding the U.K. market at the time, and the bands coming out of this scene consisted of upstarts like Iron Maiden, Def Leppard, Tygers of Pan Tang, Motörhead (even though they predated it), Samson, and Saxon. These bands would get massive coverage in my favorite British rock magazine, and their songs would regularly be listed on the sales charts. The British stuff at the time had a certain element of "class" about it—it seemed like metal was taken more seriously and treated with respect by the press. It also had a very distinct sound from the metal coming out of the United States—British metal was harder, had some great dual-guitar work, and had a high level of aggression. These new bands were taking what was laid out by their predecessors like Queen, Judas Priest, and Black Sabbath and bringing a new flair to it. Maiden, no doubt, was the biggest band to come from this scene, followed by Def Leppard—though, to this day, Def Leppard claims that they were lumped in with this movement even though they never truly identified with it. There was one band that emerged from NWOBHM that we all thought would be massive here in America: Saxon. And they came pretty darn close.

Formed in 1976, Saxon enjoyed their biggest and most successful run during the '80s in Europe. They first came on my radar around the release of their second and third albums, *Wheels of Steel* and *Strong Arm of the Law*, respectively, and to this day they are metal classics. Saxon has always been led by singer Biff Byford, and their earliest lineup fea-

tured guitarists Paul Quinn and Graham Oliver, bassist Steve Dawson, and drummer Dave Ward. Some of the band's most enduring material was created in those early years. Tracks like "747 (Strangers in the Night)," "Dallas 1 PM," "Motorcycle Man" (which Biff jammed onstage with Metallica in 2011), "Strong Arm of the Law," and "Wheels of Steel" (an amazing driving song) are not only Saxon classics but also metal classics! The production on Saxon albums always seems to jump out at you. The band helped usher in a heavier direction in metal, while still keeping a great sense of melody. You can even hear early hints of what would become thrash metal in some of their more up-tempo material.

Saxon's fourth album, *Denim and Leather*, is my favorite in their catalog. By this point, they had truly gelled as a band. They had been taken under the wing of Motörhead, whom they had shared the stage with many times, and were one of the first bands to ever play the legendary Monsters of Rock festival (now known as Download) in Donington Park, England. With a fair amount of touring under their belt, Saxon had gained confidence in their writing and performance, and it shows on this incredible record. *Denim and Leather*'s title track is the quintessential metal rallying cry, with its giant riffs and groove, and the story-driven "Princess of the Night" is easily one of the band's best-known songs from this set. I was totally into Saxon and would read up on them as much as I could. While the band had become a major player in the metal world in their native England, in America they were only really embraced by the more

LEFT: Biff Byford
OPPOSITE: Nibbs Carter, Nigel Glockler, Biff Byford, Doug Scarratt, and Paul Quinn

EDDIE'S PLAYLIST

SAXON

1. 747 (STRANGERS IN THE NIGHT)
2. HEAVY METAL THUNDER
3. POWER & THE GLORY
4. WHEELS OF STEEL
5. CRUSADER
6. STRONG ARM OF THE LAW
7. PRINCESS OF THE NIGHT
8. SAILING TO AMERICA
9. DENIM AND LEATHER
10. DALLAS 1 PM

TOP: Graham Oliver
BOTTOM: Paul Quinn, Biff Byford, Eddie, Nibbs Carter, Doug Scarratt, and Nigel Glockler

underground metal scene. But word of mouth was growing, and it seemed like only a matter of time before Saxon would be as massive stateside as they were in the U.K.

But that degree of success never came. In 1983 Saxon released *Power & the Glory* and toured the United States with Accept—and they were incredibly powerful; new drummer Nigel Glockler, who joined in 1981, was a powerhouse behind the kit. The band delivered live in a big way, but the timing always seemed to be off for their success. By '83, metal was becoming both heavier (Metallica, Megadeth) and more commercial (Def Leppard, Scorpions). Saxon seemed to fall in between these two worlds, and as much as metal radio shows like the one I started in '83 embraced the band, they still never had anything close to mainstream radio or video airplay. In many ways Saxon served as a bridge from the classic rock bands of the '70s to the harder thrash of groups like Metallica, who have cited them as an influence. Saxon never had an image or look of any kind—no gimmick, no mascot, no elaborate stage sets or props. They were just a loud, in-your-face metal band with anthemic songs and a charismatic frontman. That should have been enough, but it wasn't.

In 1984 Saxon released *Crusader*, which started to show a slightly more polished sound. It's truly a great album in hindsight, but some fans were turned off by its slicker approach, and I couldn't help thinking that the standout track on the album, "Sailing to America," was a cry for more attention from their American fan base. The lack of U.S. commercial success seemed to take its toll, resulting in Steve Dawson's leaving the band. The next two albums missed the mark—*Innocence Is No Excuse* in 1985 and *Rock the Nations* the following year. For me and many other Saxon fans, the band was pretty much done, and by the time the inevitable line-up changes began, Saxon was old news.

Saxon continued to put out numerous albums, but stopped playing in America for many years. However, in 2007 they released their best album in ages: *The Inner Sanctum*. It was a return to form and included a proper American release, so Biff came to the United States, and I had him on my radio show to promote it. It was great to see so many hard-core Saxon fans calling in that night to show their love for the band. It was clear during our interview that Biff was really moved to know that Saxon hadn't been forgotten. It gave him an extra charge to work the U.S. again, which Saxon soon did with their first American tour in decades. Even though it was a club tour, the venues were packed, and the current Saxon lineup of Byford, Quinn, and Glockler, along with bassist Nibbs Carter and guitarist Doug Scarratt, enjoyed somewhat of a rebirth. They have since followed up *Sanctum* with the equally strong releases *Into the Labyrinth*, *Call to Arms*, and *Sacrifice*, which have not only given them a career in America again but have also raised their draw and profile in Europe, where they are regulars on the festival scene.

In early 2012 I was able to book Biff on *That Metal Show*. He flew from the East Coast to Los Angeles to do the show the same day, then back east to resume a tour. He was booked as the second guest after Marilyn Manson that day. One of the things I like to do when putting together a show is to pair artists from different worlds who people wouldn't expect to be fans of each other. It often makes for some great TV moments, and I truly thought Manson and Biff would be a great combination. Manson is obviously a much bigger name in America, so VH1 determined he would be the lead guest, with Biff having the second slot. What nobody accounted for (and we should have) was that Manson was hammered on absinthe at the time of his interview. While at times funny, Manson was out of his mind. I'll never forget Manson going on and on about Biff being such a "beautiful man" and saying what a poetic metaphor "Denim and Leather" was for "keeping us all together." With Manson, it's often difficult to figure what's real and what's ballbusting. If you've watched this episode, you can see Byford doing his best to take it in stride. In a perfect world, we would have done a full hour with Biff, as I have done many times on the radio, but the TV and radio worlds have different criteria. In the end, I was just happy to give a guy who was so influential to so many, but never achieved commercial success, some TV time in the States.

SLASH

With the implosion of Guns N' Roses in the mid-'90s, you would have been well within your rights to think that the members of the original band would no longer be with us in 2013. But against all odds, they are thankfully still among the living. The stories of the band's hedonistic excesses are extremely well documented, perhaps mostly regarding their brilliant lead guitarist, Slash. For me, as a Guns fan, the band is really all about their debut, 1987's *Appetite for Destruction*. Sure, I like songs on 1991's *Use Your Illusion* albums, but other tracks started sounding a bit bloated to me around that time. I preferred the four-minute raw, loud rock songs of the debut over the lush epics that soon followed. So when Slash announced in 1994 that he was forming a new band, born out of his frustration that Guns seemed to be stalled, I was thrilled. His energy, not to mention his playing, was one of the things I most liked about Guns N' Roses. Known for his bluesy, lyrical guitar work,

CLASSIC LINEUP:

**SLASH
(GUITAR)**

DISCOGRAPHY

The first post-Guns N' Roses release from Slash was with a band called Slash's Snakepit. More a "project" than a proper band, Snakepit was formed to play a collection of songs originally intended for Guns that the guitarist had been sitting on while the band was in limbo. Their debut album, titled *It's Five O'Clock Somewhere*, came out in '95, a year before Slash officially announced his departure from Guns. Snakepit included fellow Guns members Gilby Clarke and Matt Sorum, along with singer Eric Dover (of Jellyfish) and bassist Mike Inez (of Alice in Chains). I was instantly drawn to this album. It was much closer to the street-fueled hard-rocking Guns N' Roses than what that band was starting to morph into. Guns N' Roses connections were everywhere on the album: from the writing and playing to the production team and even the record label Geffen—which may have played into a lighter level of promotion than expected. You see, Guns N' Roses was a *major* cash cow for the label. If that band's guitarist's debut solo album became a hit, especially given that tensions were so high between band members at the time, it could signal the end of GN'R. But the bluesy hard rock on *It's Five O'Clock Somewhere* still found an audience and the album did well, in part by persistent touring. To me, this was the album that GN'R should have released after *Appetite*. I especially loved singer Eric Dover, who had a gravelly urgency to his voice that really put the album over the top. *It's Five O'Clock Somewhere* remains one of my favorite Slash albums to this day.

Slash officially announced his departure from Guns N' Roses in 1996. Next up was a blues cover band called Slash's Blues Ball. They gigged for the next few years but never released a proper album. So in 1999, I was thrilled to hear that Slash was bringing Snakepit back, but this time with a new lineup that featured a new singer by the name of Rod Jackson. Dover was a huge part of what I loved about the first album—his writing and the emotion he was able to convey in his vocals were something I would surely miss. I liked Rod's voice, and the new band did a great job, but to me, their album *Ain't Life Grand* didn't pack the same punch as the first. Still, *Ain't Life Grand* certainly had some fine moments, and I was thrilled Snakepit was active once again.

I saw Slash and this band several times on tour, including dates they opened for AC/DC as well as their own shows as headliners. I had Slash and Rod in my radio studio around this time, and both guys were far from sober. That night, I caught Slash trying to make off with some of my CDs, and Rod, who I didn't know at all, asked me where he could "score"

the music landscape had even impacted his brand of bluesy hard rock. He was no longer the mysterious cool guy, and when I think back on it, he was dangerously close to being viewed as an '80s has-been. By 2002, Snakepit had ended again.

It was in 2002 that Slash, Matt Sorum, and Duff McKagan connected at a tribute show for late Ozzy Osbourne drummer Randy Castillo. The idea was born at that event for a new band with all three former Guns N' Roses members teaming up, along with guitarist Dave Kushner. Finding a singer proved difficult, and even played out on a TV reality show. Ultimately, that singer was Scott Weiland of Stone Temple Pilots, and working with him proved as difficult as deciding on him as the vocalist had been. It was hard to believe these guys, coming from Guns N' Roses and given all the complicated issues with Axl Rose, would choose another guy as enigmatic, and as notorious for his issues with the law and substance abuse. But you can never account for what will and won't click with musicians, and the band, called Velvet Revolver, soon released the single "Set Me Free" as part of the *Hulk* soundtrack. The group was immediately embraced, unlike anything else Slash, Sorum, or McKagan had done since Guns. And I think much of the credit goes to Weiland, who had major alternative hard rock cred with radio from his success in Stone Temple Pilots. Their debut, 2004's *Contraband*, entered the *Billboard* charts at number one, and their second album, 2007's *Libertad*, also had commercial success. While both records have great moments, to me, they don't have that loose energy that is such a part of Slash's sound.

And it seemed like déjà vu with Axl all over again. I attended shows where I was backstage and Weiland would not come out of his dressing room, or would be fighting inside it with his wife. It all seemed pretty intense. I recall once texting Slash while he was touring in Abu Dhabi. He confessed that things were really crazy with Weiland and that he was done with him after that run of dates. Weiland himself announced the end of the band onstage, but it was only the end of Weiland. To this day Slash,

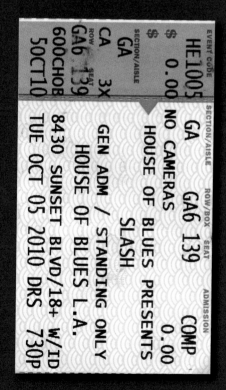

LEFT: Scott Weiland and Slash
OPPOSITE: Slash

EDDIE'S PLAYLIST

SLASH

1. BEGGARS & HANGERS-ON (SNAKEPIT)
2. BEEN THERE LATELY (SNAKEPIT)
3. DIME STORE ROCK (SNAKEPIT)
4. BACK FROM CALI
5. STARLIGHT
6. FALL TO PIECES (VELVET REVOLVER)
7. SLITHER (VELVET REVOLVER)
8. STANDING IN THE SUN
9. BY THE SWORD
10. ANASTASIA

Duff, and Sorum want to continue the band, but finding the right guy to front it has proved tough, given their busy schedules. Slash has told me that despite his current success as a solo artist, it's important to him to revisit Velvet Revolver at some point because he feels the band has unfinished business and a great album still to make. It's anyone's guess if and when that will happen.

In 2006, I worked as a producer on the VH1 show *Rock Honors*. One of my main jobs was putting together the band that paid tribute to Kiss during the show. Kiss wouldn't allow Ace Frehley to play with them, so Ace ended up playing in the tribute band with Slash, Tommy Lee, Gilby Clarke, Scott Ian, and Rob Zombie. Why did Ace do it? Because he wanted to jam with Slash. Ace had just started to get sober at the time, and I warned him that being around Slash in Vegas, where the show was to be shot, could really test him. He assured me that he would be fine. But the night before, when we were all hanging out at the House of Blues, Slash, who was not sober, tugged on my shirt and said, "Keep an eye on your buddy over there. We need him tomorrow." With that, I saw Ace dancing and swaying across the room, drinking and partying. He had failed his test, and even a drunken Slash could see it. I'm very proud to say Ace got sober for good shortly after that, as did Slash.

In 2009, Slash set out to make his own album that featured a series of guest singers. Simply called *Slash*, it featured a wide range of styles, with each guest vocalist putting his or her own lyrics and voice on music Slash had written. I paid a visit to Slash's house before the album was released, and he played me several tracks. The ones I liked most featured Alter Bridge singer Myles Kennedy, who eventually toured for the album with Slash, covering many different singers and doing a truly remarkable job. I interviewed the guys for the album and tour many times on radio and TV. Slash, admittedly, is not a self-promoter, so he counts on me to step up and make the pitch for him. He also hates seeing himself on TV. He will watch *That Metal Show*, but not the episodes he's on. Slash's live band was incredible and also featured bassist Todd Kerns (a great singer and guitarist in his own right, who I knew from a Vegas band called Sin City Sinners) and drummer Brent Fitz (from Vince Neil's band and Union). It was pretty much my favorite Slash band since the original Guns N' Roses. So I was thrilled when Slash decided to make it a real band in 2011 and even give it a name: the Conspirators. In 2012, Slash invited me to the studio while I was in L.A. to hear some tracks, and it was exactly what I'd hoped for. Even without vocals at that point, I could tell the album would be special. It featured the same guys playing on all the songs, and this made for a more cohesive experience. The album, *Apocalyptic Love*, was one of my favorites of the year.

Slash has been a great friend over the years. We often text or talk, and it's funny—although he is such a "guitar god" in his own right, when we hang out, that never enters into the conversation. Together we share stories and music from bands we both grew up loving. I truly appreciate his friendship and support for the work I have done over the years (like even taking the time to show support for this book). I also really love the guys in the Conspirators—they are great players and people and huge rock fans. When we all get to talking together, we go so far off into our own rock-geek world that often Slash gets up and walks away, just shaking his head.

Slash plays on Steven Adler's debut album, *Back from the Dead*. Listen for his solo on the song "Just Don't Ask."

ABOVE: Myles Kennedy
LEFT: Todd Kerns, Eddie, Slash, and Myles Kennedy
OPPOSITE: Slash

TESTAMENT

In 1986, I was working at Megaforce Records when Testament came to my attention. They were a young band of thrash metalers making a name for themselves in the San Francisco Bay Area. Since this was such a fertile area for thrash, it wasn't long before Testament attracted lots of interest and was signed by Johnny Z and Metal Maria at Megaforce, a small label with only a few people working out of a house in Old Bridge, New Jersey, at the time. When Megaforce was considering bands to sign, everyone would throw in their two cents before a decision was made. With Testament, I must give all credit to Metal Maria Ferrero, a legendary figure in the world of metal who to this day runs her own PR firm. Maria was a fierce advocate for Testament. She believed in this band more than anyone else at the time, and history has proved her right. You see, outside of the Big Four of thrash (Metallica, Slayer, Megadeth, and Anthrax), Testament is very much in the conversation for being in the hypothetical "Big Five."

CLASSIC LINEUP:

CHUCK BILLY (VOCALS)

GREG CHRISTIAN (BASS)

LOUIE CLEMENTE (DRUMS)

ERIC PETERSON (GUITAR)

ALEX SKOLNICK (GUITAR)

KEY ADDITIONAL MEMBERS:

JON ALLEN (DRUMS)

GLENN ALVELAIS (GUITAR)

JON DETTE (DRUMS)

STEVE DIGIORGIO (BASS)

GENE HOGLAN (DRUMS)

JAMES MURPHY (GUITAR)

STEVE SMYTH (GUITAR)

STEVE "ZETRO" SOUZA (VOCALS)

JOHN TEMPESTA (DRUMS)

OPPOSITE: Chuck Billy and Eric Peterson

DISCOGRAPHY

Testament's history goes back to 1983 in Berkeley, California, when they were formed under the name Legacy. Technically, the only band member who has been there since day one is guitarist Eric Peterson—and many musicians have come and gone throughout the decades. In '86, the band had just switched singers, enlisting Chuck Billy to replace Steve "Zetro" Souza, who had left to join fellow Bay Area thrash titans Exodus. Maria was the one who brought their tape into the office meeting where we reviewed band submissions. In all honesty, I was much more of a fan of melodic rock at the time, and Legacy was out of my area of expertise. Their music was more abrasive than the kind I loved, but I could certainly recognize their talent and how they might fit into the Megaforce world.

Once the band was signed in 1986, they quickly began recording their debut album in upstate New York with producer Alex Perialas, who had worked on many albums put out by Megaforce. The band was still called Legacy at the time the debut album was recorded, but because of some trademark issue with another band, the label's legal counsel instructed us that they couldn't use that name on the album's release. A crazy brainstorming session began to decide what they would be called. The answer came from S.O.D./M.O.D. frontman Billy Milano, who threw out the name Testament, and the rest is history.

Testament titled their debut *The Legacy* as a nod to their past moniker, and the band was embraced quickly by the rapidly growing thrash movement. *The Legacy* is a raw and heavy thrash classic that quickly caught the attention of the hard-core metal masses. Chuck Billy's huge roar grabs you by the throat and demands that you pay attention, and Peterson's riffs are crunchy as all hell. But perhaps the secret weapon in the Testament assault is the lead guitar playing of its youngest member, Alex Skolnick, who was still in his late teens at the time the album was recorded. Skolnick is a cut above some of the players in this genre of music. His fluid solos and brilliant melodies, combined with his shred

LEFT: Alex Skolnick
OPPOSITE RIGHT: Eric Peterson, Eddie,
Chuck Billy, Alex Skolnick, Gene Hoglan,
and Greg Christian
OPPOSITE LEFT: Alex Skolnick and
Greg Christian

1. PRACTICE WHAT YOU PREACH 2. DARK ROOTS OF EARTH 3. MORE THAN MEETS THE EYE 4. THE BALLAD 5. INTO THE PIT 6. DOG FACED GODS 7. TRIAL BY FIRE 8. ALONE IN THE DARK 9. THE NEW ORDER 10. RAGING WATERS

EDDIE'S PLAYLIST TESTAMENT

ABOVE: Greg Christian
OPPOSITE TOP: Chuck Billy
OPPOSITE BOTTOM: Eric Peterson

factor, really give the band's music a special quality—and are something that I personally love about the band's music. Skolnick was taught by Joe Satriani and had musical interests that went beyond metal, which would later push him to leave the band for a while. But coupled with the writing and great playing of Eric Peterson, Testament had a great guitar attack.

Soon after their debut release, Testament was touring with Anthrax and being mentioned in the same breath as the Big Four bands. With edgier metal music, it's pretty much a given that mainstream radio is not an option, so Testament had to work aggressively through the press, word of mouth, touring, and playing college and metal radio specialty shows. They were well received by all, and their live show delivered an even greater punch than their album. *The New Order* and *Practice What You Preach* followed in 1988 and 1989, respectively, each selling more copies and gaining greater ground for the band. They even scored some radio and video airplay for the tracks "Practice What You Preach," "The Ballad," and a cover of Aerosmith's "Nobody's Fault." These early Testament albums are among my favorites. The production is thin and raw, but it adds to the amazing energy and overall "thrashiness." It's great to hear this young band grow and evolve with each release and stake their claim to thrash metal greatness.

I became quick friends with the guys because they had grown up loving many of the same bands that I did, like Queen, Scorpions, UFO, Thin Lizzy, Kiss, Iron Maiden, and Aerosmith. We would often hang out for hours talking about our favorite albums. Testament had an admitted appreciation for more melodic hard rock, which they weren't afraid to show—something that was rare back in the days of speed metal, when some bands were trying to uphold a certain image. On the flip side, founding member Eric Peterson also had a love of even more extreme death metal and black metal. This creative struggle resulted in Alex Skolnick's leaving the band to spread his wings in 1993, along with drummer Louie

UNDERGROUND CLASSIC

Check out 2001's *First Strike Still Deadly*, a collection of rerecordings of material from the band's early albums. Testament was never happy with the production of their first few albums, so they decided to redo punchier versions with better sound and with John Tempesta on drums.

Clemente. Skolnick went on to form a jazz trio, join Savatage for a brief time, and then perform with Trans-Siberian Orchestra for several years. Testament then saw a revolving door of players with conflicting influences and the band experimented with musical styles. But Skolnick returned to the band on a permanent basis in 2008 with the release of *The Formation of Damnation*, a huge comeback album that in my opinion ranks among their best work.

In 2001, Chuck Billy was diagnosed with cancer after a tumor was discovered in his chest during a routine exam. Chuck never thought he would perform with Testament again, but after being sick and going through the process of recovery, he had an even greater appreciation for and rededication to the classic lineup of the band and the music they made, and his battle with cancer helped bring this group back together. Chuck revealed in a 2012 interview that he believes his cancer was cured with the help of a Native American Indian ceremony and a visit from a medicine man. He remains cancer-free and continues to be the voice of the band today.

Countless musicians have come and gone in the history of Testament, which helps explain why they don't have a higher standing in the metal hierarchy. But the respect for the band is there on a global level for their brutal brand of thrash, as well as their technical ability. In 2012 they released *Dark Roots of Earth*, which entered the *Billboard* charts in the Top 20. In addition to some great original material, the album contains bonus tracks in the form of covers of songs by Iron Maiden, Queen, and Scorpions. After thirty years, Testament continues to be one of the landmark thrash bands, creating modern classics while still giving a nod to the great bands that helped shape them. In 2013 they teamed with Overkill to tour the U.S.—two legends of the genre that both deserve more credit.

TRIUMPH

On a fairly regular basis I'm asked, "Whatever happened to Triumph?" At first glance, it appears the band has been dormant for more than twenty years (outside of a few appearances). However, on closer inspection, this much-loved Canadian trio has actually kept quite busy, though not as a touring act.

CLASSIC LINEUP:

RIK EMMETT
(GUITAR/VOCALS)

MIKE LEVINE
(BASS/KEYBOARDS)

GIL MOORE
(DRUMS/VOCALS)

KEY ADDITIONAL MEMBER:

PHIL X (GUITAR/VOCALS)

DISCOGRAPHY

Triumph's roots go back to 1975, when drummer/vocalist Gil Moore and bassist/keyboardist Mike Levine connected with guitarist/vocalist Rik Emmett on the Toronto club scene. From the start, Triumph's style of hard blazing rock was a bit more edgy and in-your-face than that of their better-known Canadian brethren, Rush—who had already started to become much more progressive—but as both were Canadian trios with prog leanings, comparisons would always be made between the two.

Triumph made their mark early with a self-titled debut album (later renamed *In the Beginning*) and quickly followed it up with *Rock & Roll Machine* and *Just a Game*. By 1979, Triumph had toured extensively in America, where they had built a strong following in Texas, Missouri, and Ohio—for some reason, certain markets' radio stations really gravitated to the band's sound, while others passed them over completely. Mike Levine, who was the band's business mind, really took note of this, and early on became Triumph's most approachable member, nurturing relationships in the business that would help crack other markets as the years went on. But it was their first attempts at rather primitive music videos (essentially, just lip-synched concert clips) that helped to introduce them to a wider American market. In 1981 MTV was just about to launch in the United States and was in desperate need of programming, so videos for Triumph songs like "Lay It on the Line" and "Hold On" from *Just a Game* were immediately placed into heavy rotation. This gave Triumph a head start on most other rock bands that were soon to be seen and heard on the channel. I can actually remember going to my friend's house, because he had MTV before I did, and just sitting there waiting for a rock video to come on. In most cases it was a Triumph clip—there simply wasn't much else available at the time!

My first Triumph album was 1980's *Progressions of Power*, which I found in the cutout bin at a now-defunct department store in New Jersey called Two Guys. Simply put, cutouts were albums that weren't selling well and had been marked down in price. In order to designate these albums as discounts that the store couldn't return to the label for full price, the corner of the album jacket was cut—thus the term "cutout." As you can imagine, the cutout bin wasn't where any artists wanted to find their records; however, many major artists had titles show up there from time to time. For me, it was a great way to discover new music with my limited allowance. That way, even if the album wasn't very good, at least I'd only paid half price for it!

I was already aware of Triumph at the time, so I took a shot and rescued a copy of *Progressions of Power*, and I really loved what I heard. The album opens with a great party anthem called "I Live for the Weekend" and also had a semi-hit that I was hearing on local radio called "I Can Survive." I immediately liked the vibe of the band, with their no-nonsense, meat-and-potatoes hard rock and a truly outstanding guitarist in Rik Emmett, who wailed all over their catchy songs. Rik also had a great voice that could go for some amazingly high notes. He was complemented by drummer Gil Moore, who also sang lead on almost half the material and had a

very cool lower register filled with attitude. Along with Levine, they were a great power trio, as they each brought something to the table.

In 1981 they released what is my favorite Triumph album, *Allied Forces*. first heard it premiered in its entirety on my local rock station, WDHA, and it practically jumped out of the speakers. For me, this is still Triumph's defining record, with its monster riffs and drums and huge-sounding songs, like the opener "Fool for Your Love," "Fight the Good Fight," and the completely kick-ass title track. *Never Surrender*, released a year later, saw the band get even bigger in America, where they soon became a full arena-rock machine and even performed on what was commonly known as "Metal Day" during the US Festival in San Bernardino, California, where they shared the stage with bands like Judas Priest and Van Halen.

On the live stage is where Triumph did the most damage. I've always been partial to two-guitar hard rock and metal bands because they have a fuller live sound, and have often felt that Triumph's sound suffered as a three-piece. But the band eventually addressed this by adding a fourth touring member who stood just offstage to play some guitar during Rik's

LEFT: Gil Moore
OPPOSITE: Rik Emmett

EDDIE'S PLAYLIST

TRIUMPH

1. BLINDING LIGHT SHOW/MOONCHILD
2. FIGHT THE GOOD FIGHT
3. ROCK & ROLL MACHINE
4. NEVER SURRENDER
5. MAGIC POWER
6. I LIVE FOR THE WEEKEND
7. FOOL FOR YOUR LOVE
8. LAY IT ON THE LINE
9. I CAN SURVIVE
10. ALLIED FORCES

solos. However, whatever was lost in the live mix, the band more than made up for with a massive stage show that featured lasers, smoke, and a talking holographic image. Once the band graduated to arenas, they became known for these elaborate productions, and lighting effects became their trademark.

As the '80s progressed, Triumph did what most bands with roots in the '70s did: They became more commercial. They tried to dress more stylishly, but as the band members themselves will tell you now, there was nothing stylish about Triumph. The result was some crazy-looking stage getups, and by 1988, the Triumph that most U.S. fans knew and loved was, for all intents and purposes, at the end. Rik began to butt heads with Gil and Mike over business and creative issues, resulting in his leaving the band later that year. This was a devastating blow to the group—not only because they'd lost one-third of their members but also because they'd lost the guy who all the girls thought was cute! Rik was the face of Triumph and basically its star. The band attempted to replace Rik with vocalist/guitarist Phil X, and even recorded an album, *Edge of Excess*, with the new lineup. However, they found themselves totally off the radar, and the band quickly disintegrated. The break between Rik and his partners in Triumph was a nasty one, driven by the fact that by leaving the band, Rik also agreed to leave a huge portion of royalties behind. You see, the band had made an agreement that if one of the three original members left, he would retain only one-ninth of his interest in the band.

After his stint in Triumph, Rik went off and reinvented himself as a jazz guitarist. Since he had such a diverse style, he even scored some hits in Canada as a solo artist. Meanwhile, Gil and Mike went behind the scenes. Gil focused on running Metalworks, the massive studio outside Toronto that he still owns. Mike, who had always run the business side for the band, schmoozing radio and industry members, kept doing exactly that. He effectively manages the band's affairs and catalog to this day, overseeing reissues and licensing of the band's songs. Because of his efforts, Triumph was the only band up until recently to own and release their '83 US Festival performance on DVD. Mike also managed to buy back the band's catalog from their old record labels and reissue enhanced versions on Triumph's own label, TRC Records.

I had Mike on my radio shows many times to promote these rereleases, and began to notice in the later years that when the question of a reunion came up, he seemed more and more open to the idea. It wasn't until 2007, however, that the real catalyst to get the guys back together came along: Triumph was inducted in the Canadian Music Hall of Fame. It was the first time in almost twenty years that Rik and his bandmates reconnected, and it led to an eventual settlement of their previous business dispute. At the very least, Gil, Rik, and Mike were friends again, and with the bad blood gone, the Triumph legacy finally felt right for us fans. With the friendship returning, the question of a reunion tour started to surface again.

Finally, it was announced that the original three members of Triumph would perform live in 2008. Only two shows were announced: one in Sweden at the Sweden Rock Festival and the other in Oklahoma at Rocklahoma, which I have hosted almost every year. Like most fans, I was thrilled at the prospect of seeing the band live once again. After I introduced them onstage at Rocklahoma, I took a golf cart and drove all the way out on the festival grounds—more than anything, I just wanted to sit in a field under the Oklahoma night sky and take in the full Triumph experience. The band was greeted warmly and sounded good, but I'd be lying if I said they were as great as they once were. Rik wasn't able to hit the high notes anymore, and there were times when they really looked and sounded like a band that had had a two-decade break. But it was still great to see them performing again, and everyone hoped it would be a springboard for a full tour. However, that was not to be. All of them have told me on my radio show that unless they saw a great demand and could play the type of venues that would allow them to put on the big productions that they were once known for, they would rather stay home. As older guys with other interests, the idea of playing small clubs just doesn't work for Triumph. Rik often plays solo club shows, but Gil and Mike are content to stay home and take care of business. In 2012 they released their show in Sweden on CD and DVD, and to this day, it stands as the band's final live

OPPOSITE TOP: Rik Emmett

W.A.S.P.

W.A.S.P. was spawned in the same early-'80s era of Los Angeles-based hard rock that produced bands like Ratt and Mötley Crüe. But few know that W.A.S.P.'s roots actually stretch back to the mid-'70s.

Blackie Lawless was born Steven Duren on Staten Island in New York City. In the mid-'70s he replaced Johnny Thunders in the New York Dolls for a few live concert dates before eventually relocating to Los Angeles. There he formed several glam-influenced hard rock bands such as Sister and Circus Circus. Sister featured a then unknown Nikki Sixx, who—borrowing some of the onstage theatrics he learned from Blackie—went on to great success in Mötley Crüe. Blackie's early bands also featured Chris Holmes and Randy Piper, who eventually became key members of W.A.S.P. Since it was first formed in 1982, W.A.S.P. has had many members in and out of its lineup, but no matter what era of the band you look at, it has always been Blackie's beast!

CLASSIC LINEUP:

CHRIS HOLMES (GUITAR)

BLACKIE LAWLESS (VOCALS/BASS)

RANDY PIPER (GUITAR)

STEVE RILEY (DRUMS)

KEY ADDITIONAL MEMBERS:

FRANKIE BANALI (DRUMS)

MIKE DUDA (BASS)

MIKE DUPKE (DRUMS)

STET HOWLAND (DRUMS)

TONY RICHARDS (DRUMS)

DARRELL ROBERTS (GUITAR)

JOHNNY ROD (BASS)

OPPOSITE: Blackie Lawless

DISCOGRAPHY

GHT: Steve Riley, Chris Holmes,
andy Piper, and Blackie Lawless
ottom)
PPOSITE: Blackie Lawless

Much of the W.A.S.P. story revolves around the outrageous "shoc
rock" elements of the band's live stage show. Early W.A.S.P. shows fe
truly dangerous at times. Adding to their menace, both Blackie Lawles
and guitarist Chris Holmes were over six foot five, without their boots
The band would have a scantily clad woman on a torture rack and tos
raw meat into the audience—along with the fire, smoke machines, an
sinister-looking stage props that were standard in heavy metal shows
W.A.S.P. combined the horror movie images of Alice Cooper with th
more comic book, superhero-oriented approach of Kiss.

Their act and sexually explicit lyrics made them prime targets of th
Parents Music Resource Center (PMRC) music censorship trials of 1985
and having a lead single titled "Animal (Fuck Like a Beast)" didn't hel
their case either. But the PMRC hearings brought the band a huge amoun
of publicity for being crude and harsh—*exactly* what young fans wante
and essentially the opposite of what the PMRC had hoped for. The PMR

also didn't know who they were dealing with. Like Twisted Sister's Dee Snider, who got a lot of press for being so articulate during the hearings, Blackie is the opposite of his image and surprised everyone by being so well-spoken. But the record label still pulled "Animal" from the band's self-titled debut over concerns that stores wouldn't put it on the shelves. This, of course, only made fans want it more, and many bought it as a single, released by an independent U.K. label. The band's visuals, along with their early anthems like "I Wanna Be Somebody" and "L.O.V.E. Machine," quickly landed them a large following, and even MTV came calling.

With the release of 1985's *The Last Command* and 1986's *Inside the Electric Circus*, their live shows grew even more elaborate, with costumes, lighting, and stage props. However, things changed in 1989, when Chris Holmes left the band—for the first time. Chris was very much viewed as Blackie's right hand in the band, and was notorious for his appearance drinking vodka while floating in a pool in the 1988 documentary *The Decline of Western Civilization Part II: The Metal Years*. The band's demanding schedule had taken its toll, and Chris, who had married former Runaways guitarist Lita Ford, was interested in spending more time with his new wife.

Following Holmes's departure, Blackie wrote and recorded what was originally intended to be a dark solo concept album, but it was released as *The Crimson Idol* under the W.A.S.P. name. Widely regarded as one of Blackie's finest musical moments, the album has been performed complete onstage on several tours since. It was the first of many very strong albums released over the past twenty years or so under Blackie's direction.

I've had a number of interactions with the band members over the years, but whenever I think of W.A.S.P., one hilarious story always comes to mind. I had just started a metal radio show in New Jersey at WDHA when W.A.S.P.'s debut album came out. In fact, one of my first interviews was with Blackie and Chris Holmes, who were trying to get some love and support for their record. I had a great visit with them that night, and just as we were wrapping up on the air, the station's owner at the time (back when radio was owned by individuals, not the huge companies of today), Bob Linder, rang the hotline. Bob invited Blackie and Chris over to his house for a hot tub party and some drinks. He said that he loved what he'd heard about the band during my interview and was very *stimulated* by the conversation. Both Blackie and Chris were excited to have the owner of the station take such an interest in them, so they happily accepted the offer. What these two hulking metal guys didn't know, however, was that they had just agreed to attend a gay hot tub party! I was unable to go with them, since I had to stay at the station, but I have heard stories from people who were there about how awkward it was for the only two straight men. But because the host was the owner of a rock station in a strong market, they wanted to make a good impression, and I give them a lot of credit for sticking around. Sadly, Bob passed away a number of years ago, but to this day Blackie and I still talk and laugh about that classic night!

EDDIE'S PLAYLIST

W.A.S.P.

1. CHAINSAW CHARLIE (MURDERS IN THE NEW MORGUE)
2. I WANNA BE SOMEBODY
3. BLIND IN TEXAS
4. WILD CHILD
5. ANIMAL (FUCK LIKE A BEAST)
6. HALLOWED GROUND
7. ON YOUR KNEES
8. 9.5.-N.A.S.T.Y.
9. CRAZY
10. L.O.V.E. MACHINE

ABOVE: Randy Piper

Being a native New Yorker, Blackie, like many, was extremely affected by the events of 9/11. He visited my radio studio a month or so after the attacks, when New York was far from recovered and the smell of the burning ruins of the Twin Towers was still in the air. I introduced him to a couple of good friends of mine who were NYPD officers, Wayne Flagg and Sean Ryan. Blackie had conversations with Wayne and Sean on and off the air about what they were going through as police officers, listening to their stories and seeing the emotion on their faces. After that visit, he wrote a moving tribute to those who lost their lives in the Twin Towers: "Hallowed Ground" appears on the 2002 release *Dying for the World*, and whenever I hear it, I go back to that horrible day and period of recovery, with the smell in the air from the rubble of the buildings. This musical turn showed that the band was not all style over substance.

I've long fought against the stereotypes of hard rock and heavy metal. People think that just by looking at someone, they can figure out the music and genre. To the uneducated, Blackie seems like a wild man. But in reality, he's extremely smart, well-spoken, and a tireless worker who is still touring the world. I asked Blackie if, as he's gotten older, it has become more difficult to perform his onstage antics, and I had to laugh when he replied, "If I wrote better songs, I wouldn't have to do this stuff." However, the truth is that Blackie has written some great songs and con-

DID YOU KNOW?

Ace Frehley and Blackie grew up together as part of a New York street gang called "The Duckies." Also, while the band's name is presented like an acronym, it has never been confirmed what this acronym really stands for.

tinues to do so. These days, because of his religious beliefs, he no longer plays "Animal" and some of the more over-the-top W.A.S.P. tunes from the early days. And now, instead of torture racks, his main stage prop is a spring-loaded mic stand, which he rides like a giant pogo stick. But do not fear, W.A.S.P. fans: The shows are just as rowdy as ever. And if you're sitting in the first few rows, you still have a good chance of getting smacked with some raw meat.

ABOVE: Blackie Lawless
LEFT: Blackie Lawless and Chris Holmes

WARRANT

My first exposure to Warrant came when I was working on the record label side of the business in the late '80s. As a young A&R scout, it was my duty to keep an eye out for hot new bands and let my boss know if there was anybody we should pursue for the label. I took a trip to Los Angeles to see two bands, Roxanne and Ferrari (led by Keel guitarist Marc Ferrari). I heard lots of buzz on that trip about a band called Warrant, who were packing clubs in Southern California and being checked out by all the majors. So I went to a venue in Reseda called the Country Club to see what the fuss was about.

CLASSIC LINEUP:

JOEY ALLEN (GUITAR)

JERRY DIXON (BASS)

JANI LANE (VOCALS/GUITAR)

STEVEN SWEET (DRUMS)

ERIK TURNER (GUITAR)

KEY ADDITIONAL MEMBERS:

JAMES KOTTAK (DRUMS)

ROBERT MASON (VOCALS)

JAIMIE ST. JAMES (VOCALS)

RICK STEIER (GUITAR)

OPPOSITE: Steven Sweet and Jani Lane

DISCOGRAPHY

Much of the L.A. scene was out in force, and I even recall sharing a table with some of the guys from another up-and-coming L.A. hard rock band called Guns N' Roses, who were about to release their debut. I knew that what I saw onstage that night could be huge and sell millions of albums, but I also knew that Warrant wasn't right for my label, Megaforce. Megaforce was more about heavier music and bands that were building via word of mouth and didn't need expensive radio promotion or elaborate videos. I also felt, to be honest, that their live performances were just average. They were good performers and had decent, catchy songs, but to me, they were just another band in a long line of West Coast commercial pop metal groups flooding the marketplace and MTV. The success they went on to have after signing with Columbia Records in 1988 didn't surprise me, but neither did the fact that it was so short-lived.

The band's history dates back to 1984, when guitarist Erik Turner started Warrant, bringing bassist Jerry Dixon on board a few months later. A variety of musicians were in and out of the early lineups, but it was the arrival of John Oswald, aka Jani Lane, that really set the band up for big success. Lane was from Ohio and was making waves with his own band called Plain Jane on the L.A. scene. In addition to Warrant's future charismatic frontman, Plain Jane also included drummer Steven Sweet. Sweet and Lane merged with Turner and Dixon, then added guitarist Joey Allen, and the classic Warrant lineup was born. Lane was more than just the voice of Warrant; he was, for the most part, the band's sole songwriter. His songs, voice, and appearance gave Warrant the magic formula of the '80s: looks and hooks.

The band's debut album was titled *Dirty Rotten Filthy Stinking Rich* and released in early 1989. Produced by Beau Hill of Ratt fame, it's a big-sounding commercial hard rock album that blends power ballads and hard rockers. Instantly, Warrant was all over MTV and scoring hits with songs like "Heaven" (the video for which featured the band in now-famous matching white leather outfits), "Down Boys," and "Big Talk." It was the definition of pop metal for the day and delivered huge sales and chart-topping success. The follow-up, 1990's *Cherry Pie*, was even bigger. Featuring the notorious title track as well as "Uncle Tom's Cabin," *Cherry Pie* shows a progression in songwriting from Lane and an overall more confident band in playing and performing. Warrant started touring with bands like Poison, Mötley Crüe, and Cinderella and seemingly overnight became a major band on the scene, driven largely by constant airplay on the world's biggest and most powerful outlet, MTV.

But by 1992, Warrant's run was already coming to an end. Because they had gotten a later start than some of the other '80s bands, they were up against the changing tide of music and were ripped a bit harder than others. Perhaps no band outside of Winger, which also had big success, was looked at more as the poster child for everything wrong with '80s music—their videos, outfits, and other rock clichés signaled to the world that grunge needed to take over. But Warrant's third album, *Dog Eat Dog*, is easily the heaviest album they made. Produced by Michael Wagener,

who had worked with Ozzy and Metallica, it has tracks like "Machine Gun" and "Hole in My Wall," whose riffs stunned me when I first heard them. But it didn't matter; by then Warrant was cooked, and although *Dog Eat Dog* was a strong record, it didn't stand a chance, being released at the same time and on the same label (Columbia) as Alice in Chains. Warrant's next few albums actually saw them chasing the grunge style, but it just buried them deeper. It's one thing to be thought of as an '80s band, but even worse to be an '80s band trying to sound modern for the times. Warrant went through a series of lineup changes and ill-fated attempts to find an audience throughout the '90s.

In 2004, Jani Lane announced he was leaving Warrant. He was replaced by former Black N Blue singer Jaimie St. James. While Jaimie did the best he could in the band—even recording a studio album called *Born Again*—without star Jani Lane, Warrant had very little chance to reclaim past glory. In 2008, Jani rejoined Warrant for a reunion tour, but it was a disaster. Lane's struggles with drugs and alcohol had not improved during his time away from Warrant, and shortly after returning to the band, he made the news by being so intoxicated at a gig in Vegas that he could barely stand during the set and was mumbling lyrics incoherently into the mic. I saw the band at Rocklahoma a couple of weeks later, when the incident was still very fresh in the band's and fans' minds, and all wondered what state Jani would be in for the show. He had been in rehab since the Vegas incident, and after intro'ing the band, I turned and saw Jani

TOP: Erik Turner and Joey Allen
BOTTOM: Eddie and Jani Lane
OPPOSITE: Joey Allen and Jani Lane

EDDIE'S PLAYLIST

WARRANT

1. SOMETIMES SHE CRIES
2. UNCLE TOM'S CABIN
3. HOLE IN MY WALL
4. MACHINE GUN
5. CHERRY PIE
6. COCAINE FREIGHT TRAIN
7. DUSTY'S REVENGE
8. MR. RAINMAKER
9. DOWN BOYS
10. I SAW RED

standing there, going through his warm-ups, seemingly fit and ready. Although he might not have been at the top of his game, he was much better than what had gone down at the Vegas show. At that same festival, a band called Big Cock was playing, fronted by singer Robert Mason. Robert is a tremendous singer and an old friend from New Jersey, who also sang for Lynch Mob and Cry of Love. Knowing that Jani's days in Warrant were numbered once again, Joey had Mason on standby, not only to possibly relieve Lane that night from his duties but also to wait in the wings as a possible full-time replacement. Shortly after that performance, it was announced that, once again, Lane was out and that Mason was Warrant's new singer.

With all respect to Jani, who had written those memorable hits and delivered them so well in his prime, I was thrilled with the arrival of Robert Mason and liked Warrant more than ever. Mason is a powerhouse singer and breathed new life and energy into Lane's now-classic songs. Jani meanwhile did some solo touring and even some shows fronting Great White. The debut Warrant album with Mason was called *Rockaholic* and released in 2011. It contains some truly great songs and production, but selling new music from any band from the '80s, especially one without its main member, is not an easy feat.

Around that same time, Warrant asked to come on *That Metal Show*, and Jani's agent contacted me and asked the same thing. The decision was ultimately VH1's, and they went with the guy who was the face of the band, Jani. Understandably, this didn't sit well with the Warrant guys, who had a new singer and an album to sell, but that's the nature of the business. In July 2011, we had Jani on the set, and as his rep had promised, he was sober and in great spirits. The only thing I noticed about him during the interview was how thin and frail he was when he gave me a hug at the end of the taping. A month later, Jani was found dead in a hotel from an apparent overdose.

I was stunned by the loss of Jani, but glad people got to see him one last time on our show having fun. A couple of months after Jani passed, I was at an appearance in Akron, Ohio, when a security guard knocked on my door and told me Jani's brother was outside and wanted to see me. Of course I said yes, and his brother came in and said that he wanted to thank me for showing Jani such respect in his last TV appearance. He said his family was grateful that Jani was on a show where his music was appreciated and he wasn't treated as just the "Cherry Pie guy" from some hair band. It meant a lot to me. Less than a year later, I finally had the current members of Warrant on *That Metal Show*, remembering Jani and talking about their future, which continues to this day with Robert Mason.

DID YOU KNOW

In addition to his guitar playing in Warrant, Joey Allen also works as an artist rep for a top music gear company.

UNDERGROUND CLASSIC

Check out the 2002 Jani Lane solo album *Back to One*. Also, *Saints of the Underground* was released in 2008 by Lane, Kerri Kelli, Robbie Crane, and Bobby Blotzer—a short-lived supergroup of sorts.

LEFT: Steven Sweet
OPPOSITE TOP: Jerry Dixon
OPPOSITE BOTTOM: Robert Mason

WHITE LION

n addition to my respect for their recording career—which was far too brief—I will fully admit that I'm including White Lion in this book because of my long history and friendship with the band's members. They were very much a part of my earliest days in the music business, and my relationship with them holds some great memories. Even now, I am constantly asked, "Whatever happened to White Lion?"

CLASSIC LINEUP:

VITO BRATTA (GUITAR)

GREG D'ANGELO (DRUMS)

JAMES LOMENZO (BASS)

MIKE TRAMP (VOCALS)

KEY ADDITIONAL MEMBERS:

NICKI CAPOZZI (DRUMS)

TOMMY CARADONNA (BASS)

JIMMY DEGRASSO (DRUMS)

FELIX ROBINSON (BASS)

DAVE SPITZ (BASS)

OPPOSITE: Mike Tramp and Vito Bratta

DISCOGRAPHY

White Lion was formed in the early '80s by Danish singer Mike Tramp and New York guitarist Vito Bratta, and they very much had a David Lee Roth-Eddie Van Halen dynamic in every sense. Tramp was the great-looking frontman, while Bratta was the serious guitar wizard. Their music was also cut from the Van Halen cloth in both style and direction—it had a great melodic quality that crossed over to many different types of fans and was a perfect fit for the MTV era. And White Lion had the musician cred, thanks to Vito, who was regarded as one of the top new players of the time. It seemed like a pairing that would last for decades, but the reality was that it lasted for only four albums.

White Lion's debut, 1985's *Fight to Survive*, is still my favorite in their catalog. *Fight to Survive* was released only in Japan, and the band struggled to find an American fan base. Their management team decided to drum up more local support, so I was sent the Japanese import, and I loved what I heard: soaring vocals, great production, good songs with power and melody, and an amazing guitar player with flash and style. I invited Tramp and Bratta to the radio show I hosted at the time, on WDHA in New Jersey. It was their first-ever radio interview, and we hit it off right from the start, exchanged numbers afterward, and soon became close friends. I also met the band's bassist, James LoMenzo, and drummer, Greg D'Angelo, and quickly bonded with them. I was convinced White Lion would be huge, and in me, they had the champion that they needed to spread the word. My radio audience loved what I played from

Fight to Survive, which soon became a hit as an import with the hard rock crowd. More and more people started coming to L'Amour, where White Lion played often, to see what all the fuss was about, and it wasn't long before the labels took notice.

In 1986, when interest in signing White Lion was intense, and I was a new hire working at Megaforce Records, I begged Megaforce owner Johnny Z to let me sign the band, but he ultimately decided to pass—Megaforce was known for putting out heavier stuff, and he didn't think the band would be a good fit. He knew that the band would need major radio support in order to break through and was worried about straying too far from the label's thrash music roots (though this would soon change with the signing of Ace Frehley and King's X, among others). Even though I was unable to sign the band, my friendship with the guys was stronger than ever. They knew I had been the first to give them a shot on the radio, and we had become friends beyond the business. Having moved from Denmark, Tramp didn't have many friends here in America early on, so he would come around to my mom's house from time to time for a home-cooked meal. Needless to say, Tramp and I were huge music fans, and we would share a meal and argue constantly about Queen, Kiss, Aerosmith, Thin Lizzy, and, of course, Van Halen!

In the end, Atlantic Records—Megaforce's distributor—ended up signing the band and releasing their second album and major-label debut, 1987's *Pride*. But the album did not come together easily. The band struggled to find the right direction during recording, and actually ended up making the entire album twice, once in Germany, and then the final version in Los Angeles with noted producer Michael Wagener.

When *Pride* first went gold, the band celebrated with a concert at the club they called home, L'Amour. They were quickly becoming a worldwide phenomenon, so everyone knew it would be one of the last times we'd see them in their old stomping ground. During the show that night, Tramp announced that *Pride* had gone gold and then went on to say that before anyone believed in White Lion, there had been one guy who was always there. To my shock, he called me onto the stage with the band, and in front of the sold-out crowd gave me my first-ever gold record! As a kid just starting out on the business side of music, this was a dream come true for me. To have a gold album was pretty much as cool as it could be, let alone to have it given to me onstage with that sort of acknowledgment! That Monday I hung it on my office wall at Megaforce and told everyone that they should have signed the band! I still have it on the wall in my home office to this day.

The *Pride* album exploded, going double platinum, with its hits "Wait," "Tell Me," and "When the Children Cry" becoming MTV favorites and Vito being recognized in the music media for his immense guitar talents. But sadly, White Lion quickly imploded. It was hard to create the follow-up fans wanted, and as a result, their third album, 1989's *Big Game*, suffered. The material was too rushed and reflected a more commercial approach. Tramp and Bratta also butted heads often, and LoMenzo and D'Angelo

ABOVE: Mike Tramp
OPPOSITE: Vito Bratta, Mike Tramp, Greg D'Angelo, and James LoMenzo

EDDIE'S PLAYLIST

WHITE LION

1. LOVE DON'T COME EASY
2. LADY OF THE VALLEY
3. CRY FOR FREEDOM
4. FAREWELL TO YOU
5. BROKEN HEART
6. LIGHTS AND THUNDER
7. ALL THE FALLEN MEN
8. FIGHT TO SURVIVE
9. LONELY NIGHTS
10. HUNGRY

TOP: Vito Bratta
BOTTOM: Eddie (far right) receiving his first gold record from White Lion at L'Amour in Brooklyn
OPPOSITE: Greg D'Angelo, Vito Bratta, Eddie, James LoMenzo, and Mike Tramp

soon became unhappy that they were not equal members of the band's business. All the songs were written by Mike and Vito (and it's worth noting what amazing songwriters they were, often producing thoughtful, socially conscious lyrics that were significant during this era of pop rock), and this created a huge disparity between their earnings. Add to this some expanding egos, and the writing was on the wall. The band's final album, 1991's *Mane Attraction*, has some great material, but by the early '90s the tide had already started to ebb away from White Lion's style of music, and LoMenzo and D'Angelo left the band before the *Mane Attraction* tour, which was not well attended. A few years later, White Lion was over.

Tramp went on to a number of other bands and solo projects and has lived all over the world. He even created a version of White Lion in which he was the sole original member, but it attracted very little interest. D'Angelo and LoMenzo played together briefly with Zakk Wylde, but LoMenzo went on to have the most high-profile gigs of any member since the band ended, playing bass with Black Label Society, Pride & Glory, David Lee Roth, Megadeth, and Ace Frehley, to name a few. He even took part in the reality TV show *The Amazing Race* in 2012.

Bratta, however, remains the biggest mystery. He was a phenomenal talent, and there's a fan base that would love to see him play again, but I know Vito well, and he's simply not interested. He still lives in the house that he grew up in on Staten Island, New York, and looks after his mom and brother. I am constantly asked, "Is it true that he works as a butcher and cut off his fingers?" Or, "Is he in bad health?" Or, "Is he broke and on the street?" All the outrageous rumors about him are 100 percent false. People have a hard time accepting that he would choose to drop out of music, but that's the case with Vito. Tramp has talked to him several times about doing a reunion, but just when it gets close to happening, things fall apart for one reason or another. Even though they created some great music together, Tramp and Bratta have always been very different people. Mike loved being a rock star and has all the swagger a frontman needs to be a success, while Vito is more quiet and reserved, preferring to keep to himself and open up only to those closest to him. While Mike is still looking for that magic moment again, Vito is content to have experienced it in his past and to move on with his life. In my own experience, I've found that some people just aren't meant to be in this business for life, and Vito—as brilliant a player as he is—is one of them. I remain friends with all of the band's members to this day, and often have discussions with them about the possibility that they could one day share a stage together again. Judging from the emails I receive, there are many who would love to see it happen, but I wouldn't hold my breath.

UNDERGROUND CLASSIC

In 2007 Rhino Records released a two-CD best-of album called *White Lion: The Definitive Rock Collection*. In addition to the band's hits, it also contains a complete 1987 live concert from the Ritz in New York City.

In 2008 Mike Tramp released an album under the White Lion name (much to Vito's disappointment) called *Return of the Pride*, although he's the only member from the classic lineup on the record. Tramp has also released several solo albums as well as an album under the band name Freak of Nature.

WHITESNAKE

To American readers, the story of Whitesnake might be somewhat surprising. By the time this British band hit American music fans' radar in the mid-'80s, Whitesnake already had a nearly ten-year history. When singer David Coverdale burst onto the radio and constant MTV rotation in 1987, many young fans had no idea the guy had been in Deep Purple! Though Whitesnake had a look and sound that very much suited what was happening in the glory days of high hair, huge guitar riffs, and big, catchy choruses, the band's roots were very, very different from those of their contemporaries.

CLASSIC LINEUP:

DAVID COVERDALE (VOCALS)

NEIL MURRAY (BASS)

COZY POWELL (DRUMS)

JOHN SYKES (GUITAR)

KEY ADDITIONAL MEMBERS:

DOUG ALDRICH (GUITAR)

TOMMY ALDRIDGE (DRUMS)

REB BEACH (GUITAR)

VIVIAN CAMPBELL (GUITAR)

MICHAEL DEVIN (BASS)

MEL GALLEY (GUITAR)

JON LORD (KEYBOARDS)

BERNIE MARSDEN (GUITAR)

MICKY MOODY (GUITAR)

RUDY SARZO (BASS)

STEVE VAI (GUITAR)

ADRIAN VANDENBERG (GUITAR)

DISCOGRAPHY

SNAKEBITE EP (1978)

TROUBLE (1978)

LOVEHUNTER (1979)

READY AN' WILLING (1980)

COME AN' GET IT (1981)

SAINTS & SINNERS (1982)

SLIDE IT IN (1984)

WHITESNAKE (1987)

SLIP OF THE TONGUE (1989)

RESTLESS HEART (1998)

GOOD TO BE BAD (2008)

FOREVERMORE (2011)

Whitesnake was indeed formed from the ashes of Deep Purple. David Coverdale had joined Deep Purple as a total unknown in 1973 and recorded three studio albums with what are commonly called the Mark III and IV lineups. Once Purple came to an end, Coverdale began a solo career and recorded two albums, *White Snake* and *Northwinds*. These early albums were barely acknowledged in the United States, but in Europe, where Deep Purple always had a higher level of notoriety, they received some attention and were supported with tours. In 1978 Coverdale decided he would take the touring band for the *White Snake* solo album and turn it into a new group. Whitesnake was born.

To track the history of Whitesnake is a fairly ambitious undertaking. Suffice it to say that there were *many* people in and out of the band from the beginning to the present day. Whitesnake may have become a

ABOVE: Bernie Marsden and Micky Moody
RIGHT: David Coverdale and Steve Vai

Whitesnake's U.S. hits "Here I Go Again," "Crying in the Rain," and "Fool for Your Loving" are actually remakes of versions from the band's early albums.

David Coverdale also has his own line of wine called Whitesnake.

band unit in 1978 in name, but make no mistake—it has always been the vehicle of David Coverdale. At one point in the early '80s, Whitesnake almost became another lineup of Deep Purple when it featured three of that band's past members: Coverdale, drummer Ian Paice, and keyboardist Jon Lord. Regardless of the members, Whitesnake in the late '70s and early '80s was very much a British blues band with hints of R&B. Look no further for proof than their first hit in the U.K., a cover of Bobby "Blue" Bland's soulful classic "Ain't No Love in the Heart of the City"; it's from Whitesnake's original EP and is still played at many of their shows. But through many band members and a string of more than a half dozen albums, Whitesnake still had not crossed over to American audiences. Some early albums were never released stateside, and U.S. tours were rare. Whitesnake, whose sound and non-pretty-boy look were considered too dated to be marketable in America, seemed destined to be relegated to the European markets.

But that all changed in 1984, when Whitesnake was signed to the powerhouse American label Geffen Records, shortly after releasing *Slide It In* in the U.K. Geffen decided to have the album remixed and partially rerecorded, and Coverdale brought in a hot new guitarist named John Sykes, who had come from the band Thin Lizzy. Sykes was younger and more from the Eddie Van Halen/Randy Rhoads school of guitar. While his playing maintained a bluesy quality that stayed true to the early Whitesnake albums, he also brought a new fire, edge, and contemporary style to the band. The remixed and rerecorded version of *Slide It In* became Whitesnake's first real American release with a major-label push behind it, and it paid off. Songs like "Love Ain't No Stranger," "Slow an' Easy," and the title track gained airplay and video play in America, firmly putting the group on U.S. rock fans' radar and appealing to a younger audience who preferred the more straight-up hard rock approach. The

ABOVE: John Sykes
LEFT: Rudy Sarzo and Adrian Vandenberg

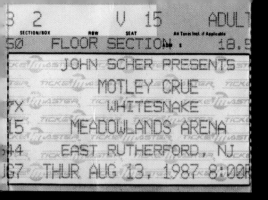

EDDIE'S PLAYLIST

WHITESNAKE

1. AIN'T NO LOVE IN THE HEART OF THE CITY
2. STEAL YOUR HEART AWAY
3. CHILDREN OF THE NIGHT
4. STILL OF THE NIGHT
5. BAD BOYS
6. LOVE AIN'T NO STRANGER
7. THE DEEPER THE LOVE
8. CRYING IN THE RAIN
9. SLOW AN' EASY
10. GAMBLER

combination of Coverdale's roaring voice and Sykes's ripping guitar had people talking, and suddenly this "new" band was very much embraced. Whitesnake entered the studio in 1987 for the follow-up to *Slide It In*, and for the first time Coverdale and Sykes wrote songs together.

The resulting album, simply called *Whitesnake* but commonly referred to as *1987*, is easily the band's biggest global hit. Everyone knew the heights to which John Sykes's playing could take the band, but the writing team of Coverdale and Sykes was truly monstrous! And suddenly Coverdale's trademark voice was all over the radio. "Still of the Night," the album's lead single, has a huge riff with Zeppelin-like swagger and big production. The *Billboard* number-one hit "Here I Go Again" epitomizes the commercial hard rock sound of the mid-'80s, and showed the band moving in a more mainstream direction, as did the power ballad "Is This Love" and its accompanying video. However, when the video for "Still of the Night" premiered, the world saw something different: The entire band, including Sykes, had been replaced by a new lineup. Shortly after recording *1987*, but before the videos were made, David Coverdale parted ways with everyone who had played on the album. In the "Still of the Night" video, drummer Tommy Aldridge, guitarists Adrian Vandenberg and Vivian Campbell, and bassist Rudy Sarzo mime the parts laid down by Sykes, bassist Neil Murray, and drummer Aynsley Dunbar.

ABOVE: David Coverdale
OPPOSITE: Vivian Campbell, Rudy Sarzo, David Coverdale, Adrian Vandenberg, and Tommy Aldridge

The lineup change didn't do anything to slow down the band's momentum. Whitesnake was still a relatively new band in America, and many had no idea that the band they saw on TV and live on tour wasn't the band they'd heard on the album (and sadly, many still don't). The biggest loss, without question, was Sykes. As a writer and a player, he was a key factor in the band's U.S. success. Sykes is one of my all-time favorite guitarists, and he and Coverdale remain friends of mine to this day. But I have never been able to get to the bottom of what went wrong at this critical stage in the band's evolution. Some feel that Sykes may have been too big a presence for Coverdale. Remember the history: Whitesnake was always about Coverdale and had been his band for more than a decade. In Sykes, Coverdale had a great-looking young guitarist who was suddenly being talked about everywhere—maybe a bit too much. It also could have come down to a business decision, which is why 95 percent of bands break up. Anyone who comes into a band like Whitesnake is going to be an employee, and that doesn't always work. I'm not taking sides either way, because I truly can't figure out how something so great ended so quickly, but it sucks to think of what could have been.

It wasn't until the *1987* follow-up, 1989's *Slip of the Tongue*, that the loss of Sykes was truly felt. More lineup changes ensued, and Steve Vai was brought in to record solos for the album, written by Coverdale and

guitarist Adrian Vandenberg. Vai is a master guitarist and technician, but I never thought this album or band was suited to him. To me, his style just didn't mesh with Whitesnake's, and he sounded more like a great player dropping in some riffs than a writer who had been a part of the music's creation. With all respect to the greatness of the players, *Slip of the Tongue* just doesn't have the same fire and attack of '87. Whitesnake continued to have success both in America and the U.K., where they headlined the 1990 Monsters of Rock festival, but they couldn't re-create the blockbuster status they'd achieved with the previous album. Shortly after the tour for *Slip of the Tongue*, Coverdale decided to take a break from Whitesnake and record an album with Jimmy Page, called *Coverdale/Page*. Outside of some reissues and a 1997 album that never saw a U.S. release, Whitesnake seemed pretty much done.

In 2000 I heard from a publicist that Coverdale wanted to come to my studio to promote a new solo album called *Into the Light*. David had been very down on the music industry, especially coming out of the '90s, when so many big bands that had been supported by MTV were being marginalized. *Into the Light* was a rock album but with a far more singer-songwriter approach than the bombast on Whitesnake releases. Coverdale was trying to reinvent himself (like most '80s icons were doing at the time). *Into the Light* was not a success on any commercial level, but it certainly got Coverdale thinking about making harder rock music again. In

most of the press for the album, he was asked the obvious question about reforming Whitesnake, and he showed very little interest in revisiting past glory. But just a few years later, Coverdale announced yet another new Whitesnake and took to the road in 2002, joined by the guitar duo of Dio guitarist Doug Aldrich and Reb Beach (previously with Winger). Coverdale was back to his screaming and strutting self, and the fans loved it. In Aldrich, David had his best right-hand guitarist and writer since Sykes. Together they have written two of the greatest Whitesnake albums since '87: 2008's *Good to Be Bad* and 2011's *Forevermore*.

Whitesnake has been active ever since. David is a true character, and I always enjoy my visits with him. We've done countless radio and TV interviews over the years, but I'll never forget my first time doing TV with him at VH1 Classic in 2004. He was in the makeup room when he heard me come in and roared out in that classic British tenor, "Edward, my dear, come and see ol' DC." He then proceeded to open a bag that contained something called "essential oils." He asked if anything ailed me, but my answer of no didn't suffice. Dr. DC reached into his bag, poured oils from various bottles into his hand, rubbed his hands together, and waved them in front of my face, pushing the scent my way. He claimed it would make for a more stimulating interview, but in all honesty, David is such a great personality and engaging guy that essential oils were never needed.

ABOVE: Reb Beach
LEFT: Vivian Campbell, David Coverdale, and Adrian Vandenberg
OPPOSITE TOP LEFT: Adrian Vandenberg
OPPOSITE TOP RIGHT: Doug Aldrich
OPPOSITE BOTTOM: John Sykes

ZAKK WYLDE

As a native of New Jersey, Zakk Wylde first came on my radar many years ago. So long ago, as a matter of fact, that he wasn't yet known as Zakk Wylde. I first knew him as Jeff Wielandt, a tall, skinny kid making some noise on the Jersey club circuit in the mid-'80s with a band called Zyris. I saw Zyris perform many times, but the band wasn't anything special outside of its dynamic, budding guitar hero named Jeff. The Zakk story really took shape when a record company guy by the name of Dave Feld approached him after a gig at a local rock club and asked him if he would ever consider auditioning for Ozzy Osbourne, since Jake E. Lee had recently left the band. Feld explained that he could get a demo tape to Ozzy through noted music photographer Mark Weiss, who was doing a session with Ozzy. Liking what he heard in Jeff, Ozzy gave him the gig and renamed him Zakk Wylde. The rest is rock history.

CLASSIC LINEUP:

**ZAKK WYLDE
(GUITAR/VOCALS)**

OPPOSITE: Zakk Wylde

DISCOGRAPHY

OPPOSITE LEFT: Zakk Wylde
OPPOSITE RIGHT: Zakk Wylde guesting
th Eddie at Q104

Zakk is a guy who worships his guitar heroes, specifically people like Randy Rhoads, Eddie Van Halen, Jimmy Page, and Jimi Hendrix. So the idea of working with an icon like Ozzy Osbourne was, and in many ways still is, almost surreal to him. He has never lost sight of being a fan first and foremost. Other important influences on Zakk's playing, which are not often discussed, are Dave DiPietro of the band T.T. Quick and Kenny Dubman of Prophet—both brilliant players who were on the New Jersey scene at the time Zakk was coming up the ranks. While mainstream success has eluded Dave and Kenny, who each have released several albums with their bands, they left a huge mark on Jeff (soon to be Zakk), and he's the first to acknowledge how important they were to him. Zakk's playing has all the influence of the guitar heroes of his day, with a nod to the Southern rock that influenced him as well. And his tone, with his trademark squeals coming off the strings, is unmistakable.

Zakk's first album with Ozzy, *No Rest for the Wicked*, was released in October 1988. It not only features Zakk's incredible playing but also gives him a co-writing credit on every track. Like Randy Rhoads and Jake E. Lee before him, Zakk became another true guitar hero in Ozzy's band and a massive contributor to his sound and songs. Zakk was the total package and quickly popped up on magazine covers everywhere, becoming a major rock star seemingly overnight. Plucking a guitar player from the clubs of New Jersey and making him an instant success is something Zakk is still grateful to Sharon and Ozzy Osbourne for. They are so close to him that he often refers to them as "Mom and Dad."

Zakk had a string of hit albums with Ozzy until 1995, when he was replaced by Joe Holmes. Zakk had become a major star in his own right by this point, and Ozzy thought it was time for some fresh blood in the band while Wylde pursued a solo career. Over this span of time with Ozzy, Zakk had changed greatly. His playing and writing certainly evolved, as did his look—from the poodle-haired, good-looking, clean-cut Jeff from Jersey to the berserker, bulked-up, biker-looking Zakk Wylde of today. His partying also got more intense, with beer drinking and hell-raising being a top priority. In one of my many radio interviews with Zakk over the years, I asked him if his transformation had gone too far. He responded, "My name is Zakk Wylde, not Zakk Mylde." Enough said.

Given Zakk's track record with Ozzy, the labels had been asking about his other projects. In 1994 Zakk had signed a deal with Geffen and debuted his first band outside of Ozzy, called Pride & Glory—a trio with former White Lion bassist James LoMenzo and drummer Brian Tichy. Pride & Glory showcased Zakk's vocals as well as his playing abilities, and the sound bridged rock, Southern rock, and metal. Many loved the band's self-titled debut album, though it wasn't a huge commercial success. Zakk followed *Pride & Glory* with something nobody saw coming: the 1996 solo album *Book of Shadows*. If *Pride & Glory* was a slightly different turn musically, *Book of Shadows* was a major curve. Mostly acoustic, and more in line with Allman Brothers and Neil Young records than anything close to heavy-ripping metal, *Book of Shadows* has gained in popularity over time

and shows an equally important side of what makes Zakk tick musically.

In 1999 Zakk returned to more familiar heavy rock territory with the launch of Black Label Society, a band (and a philosophy of sorts) that continues to be his main group to this day. The success of BLS and its growing legions of fans (easily recognizable by their BLS vests) eventually led to Zakk's second dismissal from Ozzy's band, in 2009 (Zakk had been playing with both bands). This time around, the parting was a bit rocky, with Zakk learning through the press that Ozzy had a new guitarist

EDDIE'S PLAYLIST
ZAKK WYLDE

1. HORSE CALLED WAR (PRIDE & GLORY)
2. OVERLORD
3. LIFE, BIRTH, BLOOD, DOOM
4. DOOMSDAY JESUS
5. STILLBORN
6. BLEED FOR ME
7. IN THIS RIVER
8. FUNERAL BELL
9. ALL FOR YOU
10. FIRE IT UP

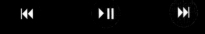

before anyone in the Osbourne camp told him he'd been sacked. The concern was that Zakk's guitar playing for Ozzy was starting to sound like his playing for BLS. That, coupled with his hard partying, meant it was time for a change. But because Zakk views the Osbournes as family, he took it all in stride and still jams with "Dad" when called upon.

I have known Zakk for a long time and truly love the guy. He knows how to have a good time, is a real music fan, and has never forgotten where he came from. But man, could he party hard in his day! I, and many others, have been around Zakk when he was hitting it hard, and—don't get me wrong—it was fun, but scary as hell at the same time. One of my most vivid memories of dealing with an out-of-his-mind Zakk is from 2005, when he released the BLS album *Mafia*. He was booked to shoot a TV interview with me at VH1 Classic, and given that I'd had so much first-hand experience with him over the years on my radio show, I knew that a serious interview was probably not in the cards. At the time, VH1 Classic was a much more conservative channel than it is now—it was scripted and full of fairly rigid interview segments. Back then, in addition to doing the interviews, I also introduced videos from all kinds of artists as a VJ. I started shooting VJ segments around one PM, and Zakk was supposed to arrive at five PM for his sit-down with me. Shortly after one, Zakk arrived, walked into the control room of the studio, and saw me introducing the video for "Dreamlover" by Mariah Carey. (Hey, a gig is a gig!) He started howling, took over the mic in the control room, and yelled, "Captain Trunk"—Zakk has a nickname for everyone—"what the hell happened to you? Mariah Carey? When did you lose your balls?" My crew looked around in horror as this boomed through the studio. I knew it would be an interesting day, to say the least.

So Zakk was asked to leave and to come back for his scheduled interview, after my other work was done. Bad move. An already hammered Zakk used the next few hours to drink more! When five PM rolled around and we were ready to shoot, it was a disaster. He showed up loaded, along with his Pride & Glory bass player James LoMenzo and Dimebag Darrell's widow, Rita. He insisted that they be in the interview, started rearranging the set, and basically unleashed all levels of mayhem at VH1. I was fully prepared for this, but the crew was not. They had never seen anything like it. Zakk was also new to his record label, Artemis, at the time, so the label reps watched in horror as this huge guy just took over and would not cooperate at all with anything! I would start out each interview take by saying, "So, Zakk, let's talk about the new album, *Mafia*," and he would pause, look at me, and say something like, "Why are you banging my wife?" Next take. "So, Zakk, how are things with Ozzy?" His reply: "You know, Captain Trunk, did anyone ever tell you that you have a dynamite ass?" Cut! Cut! Cut! The crew was becoming more panicked with each botched take. I was in a tough spot because I found it hysterical, but my boss was not laughing. So I tried to walk a line between capturing Zakk's insanity live but not encouraging it more, but I can't tell you how uncomfortable it was. To this day, it is the only interview I have ever done in more than ten years on TV that never aired! As I left the studio that day, spinning from what just went down, Zakk grabbed me in the elevator and tossed me into his waiting van, and we went to a New York City bar to continue the craziness. And trust me, I needed a few after all that. Zakk was told at the time that he was forever banned from VH1—which didn't last, of course. We have had great visits with him since on *That Metal Show*.

A huge change happened for Zakk in 2009 when he was diagnosed with blood clots. Because of the medication he needs to be on for the rest of his life, he simply cannot have any alcohol. He drinks, he dies—it's as simple as that. While difficult, it was a blessing in disguise, because Zakk might not have made it at the rate he was going. Today he is totally sober and doesn't remember the above story (or countless others). But while Zakk Wylde is a changed man, he is still a monster talent, and will always be a blast to hang with.

ABOVE: Zakk Wylde
OPPOSITE RIGHT: Zakk Wylde
OPPOSITE TOP LEFT: Nick Catanese
OPPOSITE BOTTOM LEFT: John DeServio

Y&T

Y &T is easily one of my all-time favorite hard rock bands. I have seen them live countless times, and they almost never disappoint. My earliest recollection of the band was from the British rock magazines I would read all the time as a kid. Even though Y&T originally hailed from Oakland, California, their history is that of a '70s band heavily influenced by British rock giants like Led Zeppelin, Cream, and the Who. Because of this, they were more embraced in the U.K. than here in the United States during their early years. It wasn't until the mid-'80s that Y&T finally broke through to a stateside audience.

CLASSIC LINEUP:

JOEY ALVES (GUITAR)

LEONARD HAZE (DRUMS)

PHIL KENNEMORE (BASS)

DAVE MENIKETTI (GUITAR/VOCALS)

KEY ADDITIONAL MEMBERS:

STEF BURNS (GUITAR)

JIMMY DEGRASSO (DRUMS)

BRAD LANG (BASS)

JOHN NYMANN (GUITAR)

MIKE VANDERHULE (DRUMS)

OPPOSITE: Dave Meniketti
and Phil Kennemore

DISCOGRAPHY

The band formed in 1974 under the name Yesterday & Today (taken from the title of a Beatles album), with the lineup of guitarist Joey Alves, guitarist/vocalist Dave Meniketti, drummer Leonard Haze, and bassist Phil Kennemore. Soon after they formed, Yesterday & Today was signed to U.K. label London Records (perhaps another reason for their strong British following) and put out two albums that were somewhat difficult to come by in America: their 1976 self-titled debut and 1978's *Struck Down*. Although these are solid hard rock albums with some truly great songs, they only scratched the surface of delivering the ferocious heavy rock the band was soon to become known for under the shortened name Y&T. (Their new, shorter name provided a nice logo and separated them from the Beatles reference.)

Their debut as Y&T, 1981's *Earthshaker*, featured a much heavier sound, which was quickly embraced in metal circles. *Earthshaker* wasn't a commercial success in America, but the British press loved it, and the band began touring in the U.K. on a fairly regular basis. Although *Earthshaker*, to this day, has some of Y&T's best songs, its production wasn't that great. So for 1982's *Black Tiger*, the band enlisted noted producer Max Norman, who had just come off a huge success with Ozzy Osbourne. With Norman's help, Y&T finally had the whole package: great songs, performances, and production.

Y&T was fantastic live, and when they were touring in the United States, I would do anything to see them. Back in those days, the legendary rock club L'Amour in Brooklyn was my mecca for seeing the bands I loved. The only problem was that I was still a kid living at home who had just gotten his license, and my incredibly paranoid Italian mom (who *still* worries to this day) wasn't thrilled by the idea of her son driving from our home in New Jersey all the way to New York City to see a rock band in a club. Making matters worse, headliners at L'Amour, which Y&T were a

the time, didn't go on until around 1:30 AM! However, I was eighteen and skillfully played the "I'm an adult now" card with Mom so I could make the trip. I can remember it like it was yesterday: leaving L'Amour at 3:30 AM, hoping my car was still there (thefts were fairly common in that area at the time), and walking into my house around 5 AM, just as the sun was coming up. My ears were ringing from the insane volume in the club as I prayed that my mother wouldn't hear me coming in at that hour. More often than not, she did hear me, and would scream louder than any Dave Meniketti guitar solo, "What could you possibly have been doing 'til this hour?" The truth? I was just seeing one of my favorite bands.

In 1983, Y&T released *Mean Streak*, another killer album, which featured a title track that finally saw some MTV support. For the band to have released three strong albums in a row was a real achievement at the time; however, mainstream success still eluded them. They were certainly garnering more attention, but as great as their albums were, none of them had produced a hit. By this time, I was just starting out in radio, and I made it my personal mission to spread the word about Y&T. I even took the initiative to contact their manager, introduce myself, and let him know that I was happy to help promote them in New Jersey through my new radio show.

The following year saw the release of Y&T's next album, *In Rock We Trust*. Although it was another solid heavy rock album, you began to get the sense that the group was starting to cave in to the pressure to produce a hit. The production was just a little too slick and refined, and for the first time, they worked with an outside songwriter. It also marked the debut of their mascot, "Rock," a cartoon robot that was featured on the album's cover and would come out onstage during performances, much like Iron Maiden's "Eddie." The combination of a more commercial sound and what I viewed as a very corny gimmick started to worry some fans.

LEFT: John Nymann and Dave Meniketti
ABOVE: John Nymann and Brad Lang
OPPOSITE RIGHT: Joey Alves, Leonard Haze, Dave Meniketti, and Phil Kennemore
OPPOSITE LEFT: Brad Lang, Mike Vanderhule, Dave Meniketti, and John Nymann presenting Eddie with a birthday cake in 2011

EDDIE'S PLAYLIST

Y&T

1. STRAIGHT THRU THE HEART
2. MIDNIGHT IN TOKYO
3. I BELIEVE IN YOU
4. BLACK TIGER
5. DIRTY GIRL
6. DON'T STOP RUNNIN'
7. WINDS OF CHANGE
8. MEAN STREAK
9. RESCUE ME
10. FOREVER

TOP: Joey Alves and Phil Kennemore
BOTTOM: Dave Meniketti and Brad Lang

Y&T had always been a very straight-up, no-frills hard rock band—one of the best—and to many fans, the changes felt both forced and calculated.

That said, *In Rock We Trust* went on to become the band's biggest-selling album to date, with semi-hits like "Lipstick & Leather" and "Don't Stop Runnin'." A live album, *Open Fire*, and an MTV concert followed in 1985, and yes, "Rock" made his appearance. Y&T was still a potent live band, but it was clear they were chasing the '80s look and sound of the MTV era, creating a bigger stage show and even starting to dress up in glam fashion. *Open Fire* also included a new studio-recorded song called "Summertime Girls," which proved to be hugely pivotal. In "Summertime Girls," Y&T finally had the massive radio hit that had so far eluded them, but it came at the expense of their hard-core heavy rock fan base. While catchy as hell, "Summertime Girls" was essentially a commercial pop rock song. It was a blessing and a curse, bringing an all-new audience and radio awareness for the band, but leaving the metal base crushed. "Summertime Girls" was included on the band's next studio album as well, 1985's *Down for the Count*. For me, this was the first bad Y&T album, and I completely lost faith in the band. With less-than-stellar songs and production, and with a back cover featuring the band wearing ridiculous outfits, fans felt the sellout was complete.

Struggles within the band also began. As a group, Y&T had a fairly

legendary reputation for hard partying, and this quickly began to take its toll. Drummer Leonard Haze, a monster player with a legendary kick drum, was the first to go, in 1986, and was quickly replaced by Jimmy DeGrasso. The band released *Contagious* in 1987, and it was the first album not only with DeGrasso but also on their new label, Geffen. Although far better than *Down for the Count*, *Contagious* was still too slick and again featured outside writers. The album's title track was the single, complete with a huge Bon Jovi-esque chorus.

Around this time, I was working for Megaforce Records and had just signed Ace Frehley. While looking for bands to pair Ace up with on his first solo tour, an agent suggested Y&T, and I was quick to agree to the idea. Despite being down on the band, I couldn't deny that they were still great live, and the idea of Meniketti and Frehley sharing a stage was extremely exciting. The lineup of Ace, Y&T, and Faster Pussycat was announced, and I made sure to venture many times to see that tour.

Unfortunately, more changes were on the horizon for the band. Long-time guitarist Joey Alves departed in '89 and was replaced by Stef Burns. Following this was another album for Geffen, 1990's *Ten*. It was a solid album, but it didn't produce any real hits, and Y&T quickly started to fall apart. Many people associated the band with the mid-'80s, but the truth was that by 1991, they had been at it for seventeen years and had achieved only moderate success, so they finally called it quits.

LEFT: Phil Kennemore
TOP: Dave Meniketti and Mike Vanderhule
BOTTOM: John Nymann and Brad Lang

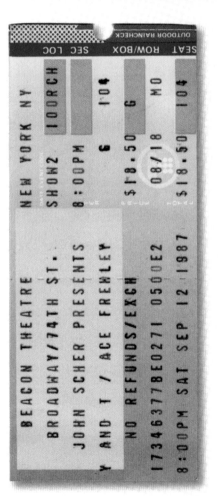

It wasn't until about ten years later, in 2001, that Y&T got their second chance: They announced they would reunite for some live shows. Guitarist/vocalist Dave Meniketti decided to return to the band, having released a few blues albums under his own name in the interim years. Drummer Leonard Haze was also back for the reunion, and joining them on second guitar was John Nymann, who, in addition to occasionally playing with the band on tours, had also worn the robot costume on more than one occasion! It seemed that everything was set, and I was excited to see Y&T perform again, especially with Haze, who had been a huge part of their sound. Unfortunately, the shows I saw were largely disappointing—it was clear that Leonard, once a thunderous, driving force for the band, simply didn't have it anymore. The years had obviously taken their toll, and this resulted in some bad live performances. Unsurprisingly, in 2006 Haze was replaced by current drummer Mike Vanderhule.

In 2010, Y&T released a new album called *Facemelter*. It was a return to their no-nonsense hard rock roots, with all the hallmarks of what made the band great: catchy hard rock with Meniketti's wailing, blues-laced guitar work and incredible voice, along with the incredible harmony vocals of Phil Kennemore (always a Y&T trademark), who wrote many of the album's lyrics. It had been a long time coming for a new Y&T album that had the band sounding so strong. The tour for *Facemelter* brought the band to New York, and I hosted their show at the B.B. King Blues Club in Times Square. Backstage, I got the chance to catch up with Phil, who mentioned that he was in a lot of pain on the road and was experiencing back issues that made it hard for him to travel. The band eventually sent him home to Northern California to get checked out, using bassist Brad Lang to finish the tour. Unfortunately, the news on Phil was not good—his doctor diagnosed him with lung cancer. Phil had smoked for almost his entire life, and in the end, it seemed to have caught up with him. He passed away just months later, in January 2011, at the age of fifty-seven. Prior to his passing, a charity concert and an online auction were arranged to help offset his medical expenses, and I offered front-row tickets to a taping of *That Metal Show* as part of a package for the auction. I wanted to do whatever I could to help Phil and his family, but he was taken away faster than anyone anticipated. I always liked talking to Phil. I think that he still saw me as the young kid who used to drive from New Jersey to Brooklyn to see his band and that he was genuinely proud of my success in the business and my continual support for Y&T. His death was very sad, especially for Dave Meniketti, who had never performed without his bass-playing partner.

But Y&T continued on and made Brad Lang an official member. Even though only Dave remains from the original band, it still feels and sounds like Y&T, largely because Meniketti remains a brilliant guitarist and singer, even after all these years. Under his leadership, Y&T is back to being that truly crushing live band I would drive at all hours to see—they're just a little older now with, thankfully, earlier start times in the clubs they play today.

LEFT: Dave Meniketti

MORE ESSENTIALS

BADLANDS

Jake E. Lee's first post-Ozzy band was a monster—with bluesy hard rock and stellar vocals from the late Ray Gillen. Sadly, it all ended after just three albums, but what is out there is truly worth a listen. Jake E. Lee's fans have long hoped for a return from the reclusive guitarist, who has been living in Vegas for the past twenty years. And in 2012 I reconnected with Jake and even had him do a walk-on during a *That Metal Show* special. In 2013 he announced his intention to return to recording and touring with a new band called Red Dragon Cartel.
Essential Album: *Badlands*

CONEY HATCH

A phenomenal melodic hard rock act from Toronto, Coney Hatch released three major-label albums and even toured with Iron Maiden. But despite some MTV airplay and a few semi-hits, they never broke through in the United States. Guitarist/vocalist Carl Dixon had one of the best hard rock voices in the business, and bassist/vocalist Andy Curran delivered his vocals with a snotty edge, giving Coney Hatch a great balance of melody and attitude. Add in Steve Shelski's slashing guitar riffs and you are left to wonder what could have been. In 2013 they regrouped for a new album, so maybe the world will have another shot to hear what they missed first time around.
Essential Album: *Outta Hand*

FASTER PUSSYCAT

Faster Pussycat was poised to be the next big breakout sleaze-rock band from Southern California. They had a fair amount of success in the late '80s and scored their biggest hit with the ballad "House of Pain." Inevitable shifts in the musical climate and many lineup changes impacted the band, leaving them to be led by singer Taime Downe, the sole original member. Taime was a huge fixture in the L.A. rock scene, not only as the singer in Faster Pussycat but also as the co-owner of legendary rock hangout the Cathouse.
Essential Album: *Faster Pussycat*

HANOI ROCKS/ MICHAEL MONROE

One of the early architects of the glam look, Hanoi Rocks and their flamboyant singer Michael Monroe burst onto the U.S. scene in the early '80s from Finland. Even though Monroe was full-on glam, he and the band possessed an attitude and a punk edge that made them well loved by many. Hanoi Rocks was so influential that Gun N' Roses reissued the band's catalog on their own label and often jammed with them. In 2011 Monroe made a commitment to remain a full-time solo artist after drifting in and out of bands with past Hanoi members over the years.
Essential Album: *Sensory Overdrive* (Michael Monroe)

ICED EARTH

Led by guitarist Jon Schaffer, Iced Earth has built a solid following in Europe and the United States with their powerful, no-frills metal. The band is Schaffer's vehicle and has featured many musicians since first coming on the scene. Schaffer is an astute student of history, and his albums often reflect his passion for the subject. He teamed with former Judas Priest vocalist Tim Ripper Owens for the album *The Glorious Burden*, which remains my favorite release in Iced Earth's impressive catalog.
Essential Album: *The Glorious Burden*

RICHIE KOTZEN

Known as a guitar shredder when he first burst onto the scene as a teenager, Richie Kotzen is so much more. Kotzen was a brief member of Poison and Mr. Big, but his all-around ability is best showcased on his solo albums, which offer an array of hard rock, ballads, blues, fusion, and a touch of R&B. An equally strong singer and player, he is often the only musician on his albums, which he also writes and produces in his home studio. I truly feel that Kotzen is one of music's best-kept secrets and one of the greatest talents I have ever seen. In 2012, I hooked him up with drummer Mike Portnoy and bassist Billy Sheehan to birth a new band called the Winery Dogs.
Essential Album: *Into the Black*

KROKUS

Many forget just how popular this Swiss-based metal band was in the early '80s. Krokus scored several hit singles and videos that saw major rotation on MTV, and singer Marc Storace was once a candidate to replace Bon Scott in AC/DC, but declined the audition to focus on his own band. As the '80s progressed, Krokus became more slick and commercial but still made solid music. The band is largely inactive in the United States these days because there isn't enough demand for live shows to offset the cost of touring, but Krokus still releases new music and plays in Europe.

Essential Album: *Headhunter*

L.A. GUNS

Though they were poised for massive success in the '80s, L.A. Guns never went over the top. The core of the band was early Guns N' Roses member Tracii Guns and British vocalist Phil Lewis—I was immediately drawn to how Phil's English snarl and Tracii's Hollywood-sleaze riffs perfectly fit together. Years of lineup changes and infighting resulted in two competing versions of the band in the 2000s, one led by Lewis, the other by Guns (with a revolving door of singers). Today's L.A. Guns with Phil Lewis and Steve Riley remains a potent live band.

Essential Album: *L.A. Guns*

LIVING COLOUR

New York City legends who combined funk, R&B, pop, and heavy rock to create a unique and powerful sound, Living Colour were the darlings of MTV with their huge hit "Cult of Personality." Known for extremely energetic live shows and featuring guitar hero Vernon Reid, the band continues to release albums with their unique blend of hard rock, and they celebrated the twenty-fifth anniversary of their debut album, *Vivid*, in 2013 by playing it live in its entirety.

Essential Album: *Vivid*

LOUDNESS

Guitarist Akira Takasaki of Loudness is the Japanese Eddie Van Halen. He is very much the star of this band, with his amazing fretboard fireworks and live energy. Loudness sang in Japanese before they got a U.S. deal in the mid-'80s, and then started singing in broken English. They scored a massively popular metal anthem that lived on MTV for many months called "Crazy Nights." In recent years they have primarily recorded and toured in Japan and have become a much heavier group that borders on thrash.

Essential Album: *Thunder in the East*

MERCYFUL FATE/ KING DIAMOND

Mercyful Fate and their lead singer, King Diamond, were massively influential with the more extreme segments of the metal world. Their riffs and musicianship, combined with dark images and lyrics dealing with the occult, had a major influence on thrash and death metal acts. King Diamond is known for his incredibly high-ranging vocal style and his full face of makeup, which at one time had to be altered because of its similarities to Gene Simmons's makeup design. Although I've never been a fan of this vocal style, I respect the quality of the music and the impact it has had on so many artists.

Essential Album: *Don't Break the Oath*

METAL CHURCH

Hailing from Seattle, Metal Church had a sound that fell between classic metal and thrash. For a time, they were embraced by both worlds, but the band had trouble maintaining a stable lineup and often toured with a revolving door of members. They ended in the 2000s, but in 2012 came together for a reunion show on a metal-themed cruise. Hopes are high that this once-great band will finally get its due.

Essential Album: *Metal Church*

MR. BIG

Best known for the huge hit ballad "To Be with You," Mr. Big combined virtuoso playing with commercial rock songs. Highlighted by bass master Billy Sheehan and guitarist Paul Gilbert, they enjoyed a string of successful albums and hits. But infighting derailed this band for many years, until they returned with a stellar album called *What If . . .* in 2011. Truly a global band, Mr. Big still fills arenas outside the United States.

Essential Album: *Mr. Big*

PROPHET

Like T.T. Quick, Prophet was on the Jersey rock scene when I was growing up. But unlike T.T., this band was far more progressive leaning, cast in the image of Pink Floyd. Incredible vocals and harmonies, stellar musicianship, and brilliant guitar work by Ken Dubman were the band's trademarks. I was so blown away by their live show that I signed them to Megaforce Records and released their second album, *Cycle of the Moon*. Prophet failed to find a large audience outside New Jersey and ultimately disbanded, but they still play in various cover bands and even did a reunion show in 2012.

Essential Album: *Cycle of the Moon*

RAVEN

Criminally overlooked when the New Wave of British Heavy Metal is discussed, this trio, led by the Gallagher brothers (bassist/vocalist John and guitarist Mark), were known for their over-the-top stage performances. Drummer Rob "Wacko" Hunter was so nuts that he wore hockey gear while playing and often lit his helmet on fire. Raven was a bridge between heavy metal and thrash, and even co-headlined a club tour with Metallica, with whom they were often mentioned in the same breath as rising metal giants. Unfortunately Raven made the mistake of going too commercial in their look and sound and alienating much of their fan base. But they still do the occasional gig and in 2013 played a benefit show for victims of Hurricane Sandy in New Jersey.

Essential Album: *All for One*

SAIGON KICK

Saigon Kick emerged from Florida ahead of their time. Sadly lumped in with the hair metal bands of the day, they showcased layers of harmonies over massive guitar riffs and were more in line with Alice in Chains than with Winger. Saigon Kick signed with a label owned by actor Michael Douglas and scored a huge hit with a ballad called "Love Is on the Way" from their second album, 1992's *The Lizard*. Shortly after, the band splintered, but they announced an original-lineup reunion tour in 2013.

Essential Album: *Saigon Kick*

SAVATAGE

Hailing from Tampa, Florida, Savatage was known for the amazing vocal wail of singer Jon Oliva and the blazing guitar playing of his brother, Criss. They began as a power metal band on an independent label before signing to Atlantic. But tragedy struck when Criss was killed in an auto accident. Shortly after, Jon decided not to continue touring with the band. Savatage went through several lineup changes and morphed into a more progressive-leaning conceptual act before disbanding completely and being folded into the massively popular Trans-Siberian Orchestra.

Essential Album: *Half of the Mountain King*

SOUNDGARDEN

Maybe my favorite of the Seattle grunge bands (along with Alice in Chains) and certainly one of the heaviest, Soundgarden channeled the brutality of Sabbath in the massive riffs of Kim Thayil and the amazing roar of Chris Cornell. Cornell possesses one of rock's greatest sets of pipes. He even once took a request from me backstage at a gig in New York for one of my favorite songs, "Fell on Black Days," and belted it out minutes later, effortlessly. I was thrilled to see Soundgarden relaunch in 2012 and release a solid new album called *King Animal*.

Essential Album: *Superunknown*

STRYPER

Those in the metal world who ridicule Stryper for their Christian leanings are selling themselves short on an amazingly talented band with some of the finest vocals and harmonies (strengthened from singing in church) that you will ever hear in hard rock music. Led by guitarist/vocalist Michael Sweet, Stryper has to be seen live to be fully appreciated. Michael, drummer Robert Sweet (his brother), guitarist Oz Fox, and bassist Tim Gaines sing and play in a lock-step unison that is truly awe-inspiring. I've always found it strange that some metal fans have an issue with Stryper singing about God but are fine with other bands preaching about the devil. Michael is such a powerhouse that he sang lead in the band Boston for a while—whose legendary vocals are no small feat to re-create.

Essential Album: *Soldiers Under Command*

T.T. QUICK

An extremely popular band on the New Jersey club scene in the early '80s, T.T. Quick was originally a cover band specializing in AC/DC. They were signed to Megaforce/Island Records and released the true underground classic *Metal of Honor*—a must for any metal fan! Guitarist Dave DiPietro is a truly underrated guitar player and had a major influence on up-and-coming Jersey rockers like Zakk Wylde, Scotti Hill, and Snake Sabo. These days, T.T. Quick singer Mark Tornillo fronts Accept.

Essential Album: *Metal of Honor*

WINGER

Perhaps no band was hit harder with the MTV backlash than Winger. The band and its leader, Kip Winger, saw their logo worn by the uncool Stewart on *Beavis and Butt-Head*, and Metallica threw darts at a Winger poster in one of their videos. Why Winger took so much of a beating is still a mystery. Sure, the band had all the trappings of the day and the image that went with it, but they were also supremely talented musicians, more so than many in that world at the time. The band had massive hits and video play before the change in music and the arrival of the MTV cartoon that crushed them. These days, Winger is regarded more for their talent and still tours and records from time to time. Kip also composes classical music, and guitarist Reb Beach plays in Whitesnake.

Essential Album: *Winger*

ZEBRA

A Long island, New York, club staple in the late '70s and early '80s (by way of New Orleans), Zebra was a power trio cast in the image of Led Zeppelin. Guitarist/vocalist Randy Jackson's incredible high falsetto is one of the band's trademarks, and he even performs in a Zeppelin tribute band along with bassist Felix Hanemann. Zebra came out at the dawn of MTV and benefited greatly from it with a hit single and video for the epic "Who's Behind the Door?" However, after releasing a few albums, the band's members went their own ways. Zebra is still based in Long Island and reunites occasionally for live shows.

Essential Album: *Zebra*

ROB ZOMBIE

One of the great entertainers and live performers of the '90s, Rob Zombie has been pushing the envelope with his sound and stage show for a few decades now. Also a successful film director, he puts all the money from his music career into his live shows. And you can see it onstage. His high energy and the robots, fire, and screen images flashing precisely to the beats of his always-stellar backing band—led by the phenomenal John 5—are all Zombie signatures. I first saw Rob with White Zombie on the New York club scene in now-extinct clubs like L'Amour and the Cat Club. With his commitment to performance and music, it's not surprising that he's outlasted many of the original venues where he got his start.

Essential Album: *Astro-Creep 2000* (White Zombie)

PHOTO CREDITS

RON AKIYAMA 4, 5, 8 (middle left & right), 10, 12, 14, 15 (left), 22, 24, 25 (left), 26, 27, 28, 31, 33, 34, 35, 38 (right), 39 (right), 40, 41, 42, 44, 45, 46, 47 (left), 48, 50, 52 (top), 59, 60, 62 (left), 63, 64, 65, 66, 68 (left), 69 (right), 70 (bottom), 71, 72, 74, 75, 76, 77, 78, 81, 82, 84, 85, 92, 96, 99, 100, 102, 103, 104, 105, 106, 109 (bottom), 111, 118, 120, 121, 122 (bottom), 124, 125 (left), 126, 128, 130, 131 (right), 132, 134, 135, 137, 138, 141, 142, 143, 144 (right), 146, 148 (right), 150, 152, 154, 155 (bottom), 157, 158, 160, 161, 162, 163, 176, 179, 180, 181, 182, 184, 185, 188, 191, 192, 194, 197, 198, 199 (right), 204, 206, 208, 209, 210, 211, 212, 214 (right), 218, 219 (right), 220, 223, 224 (top left & bottom), 225, 229 (right), 231 (top right & bottom)

GENE AMBO 54, 56 (right), 57 (left), 58 (bottom)

KEVIN BALDES 36

MARK BROOKE 6 (top left), 8 (bottom left), 9 (top right)

JEANNE GALARNEAU 30

BOB GRUEN 164

KEVIN HODAPP 8 (top left), 68 (right), 69 (left), 108, 109 (top), 112, 115 (right), 116, 117, 122 (top), 123, 144 (top left & bottom), 145, 166, 167 (right), 168 (left), 170, 174 (top), 175, 186, 187, 190, 224 (right), 230 (top), 231 (left), 233, 240

GUIDO KARP/MAGIC CIRCLE ENTERTAINMENT 114, 115 (left)

GENE KIRKLAND 94

JILL MENIKETTI 226, 228, 229 (left), 230 (bottom)

TAMARA SINGER 16, 19, 20 (bottom)

RON SOBOL 155 (top), 156, 215 (right)

KAI SWILLUS 172

LAURENS VAN HOUTEN/FRANK WHITE PHOTO AGENCY 95, 97, 98

MARK WEISS 6 (right), 7, 18 (left), 20 (top), 21, 38 (left), 39 (left), 51, 53, 90 (right), 151, 173, 196, 199 (left)

FRANK WHITE 18 (right), 56 (left), 57 (right), 58 (top), 62 (right), 86, 88, 89, 91, 129, 167 (left), 168 (right), 178, 200, 202, 203 (top), 205, 214 (left), 215 (left), 216, 217, 219 (left)

All other photos courtesy of
EDDIE TRUNK

DEDICATION

This book is dedicated to my family. I want to thank my mom and dad, Ray and Rose Trunk, and my brother, Greg, for their endless love and support as I pursued my rock obsession. And to my "other mother," Aunt Pauline Falcone—to say she has always been there for me would be the greatest understatement of all. RIP, Uncle Vince Falcone, who I still miss every day. And thanks to my wife, Jennifer, for her continual support and understanding, and to my kids, Raymond and Elizabeth, who are the greatest love I have ever known.

ACKNOWLEDGMENTS

Thanks to my editor, Tamar Brazis, for her tremendous work and assistance on this book and for helping me to get it done, and to Danny Maloney for his brilliant design work. To Amy Franklin and all at Abrams—thank you!

Thanks to John Pasquale and all those at my home away from home, the Hard Rock Cafe in NYC.

Thank you to my partners on *That Metal Show*, Jim Florentine and Don Jamieson. Always great laughs!

Thanks to everyone at VH1/VH1 Classic for twelve great years and many more.

Thanks to all those outlets that carry my radio shows, especially my NYC flagship, Q104.3. Thanks to Larry Kahn, Maria Musaitef, Justin Yuen, Andrew Ramsingh, and Katy Irizarry for their help in radio. And thanks to the "Trunk Nation" on SiriusXM.

Thanks to my attorney, Rick Meuser. Thanks and appreciation to Erik Luftglass, Andy Gershon, and David Souza.

Thanks to Brad White and all at CEU.

Thank you to my friend and photographer, Ron Akiyama, and to all the great photographers who have lent their talents and photos to this book. And to Eric McConnell, who took the photo on the last page of my first book (of Gene Simmons breathing fire)—he was mistakenly uncredited and has busted Ron's balls every day since. You finally got your credit!

And most of all thanks to YOU, for buying my books, reading, listening, and watching.

Editor: Tamar Brazis
Designer: Danny Maloney
Production Manager: True Sims

Library of Congress Control Number: 2013936552

ISBN: 978-1-4197-0869-5

Printed and bound in the United States

10 9 8 7 6 5 4 3 2 1

Abrams Image books are available at special discounts
when purchased in quantity for premiums and promo-
tions as well as fundraising or educational use. Special
editions can also be created to specification. For detail
contact specialsales@abramsbooks.com or the address